MA
MINORCA

Jack Altman

JPMGUIDES

Contents

- **Majorca and Minorca** — 3
- **Flashback** — 7
- **On the Scene** — 15
  - *Majorca* — 15
  - *Minorca* — 39
- **Balearics from A to Z** — 50
- **Shopping** — 52
- **Sports** — 54
- **Dining Out** — 56
- **The Hard Facts** — 59
- *Index* — 64

Map
- Mahón — 63

Fold-out map
- Majorca
- Minorca
- Palma de Mallorca

Majorca & Minorca

The natural beauties of the two islands are striking enough to resist all the onslaughts of modern development. Though quite dissimilar, they both have rugged charms that go far beyond what might otherwise be the appeal of mere sand, sea and sun. Standing affirmatively aloof off Spain's east coast, they derive their names from the Romans' *Balearis Major* and *Balearis Minor,* largest and second largest of the archipelago, completed to the south by Ibiza and tiny Formentera.

Under the post-Franco Spanish constitution, the Balearic Islands have formed an autonomous administrative community since 1983, with its local government in Palma, capital of Majorca. The first road signs you see are likely to proclaim the new regional pride. Black graffiti systematically alter the national (Spanish) version of place names to those of the local, Catalan-based dialect —from Puerto to *Porto,* from Mahón to *Maó.*

The Big One

Majorca covers an area of 3,640 sq km (1,405 sq miles) for a population of more than 800,000. It has long attracted the rich and famous: Austrian archdukes, Britain's Prince Charles, French novelist George Sand and her beloved composer Frédéric Chopin, other writers like Robert Graves and Jorge Luis Borges, and a galaxy of showbiz stars from Charlie Chaplin, Errol Flynn and Ava Gardner to John Lennon and more recently Michael Douglas and Catherine Zeta Jones. They were onto a good thing.

Most holidaymakers are initially drawn by the white sandy beaches or more secluded spots tucked in among towering cliffs. The main concentration of resort hotels is on the sprawling strands flanking Palma. Other white sand beaches are located over on the northeast coast at Alcúdia and Ca'n Picafort. Elsewhere, the coast is more rugged. In the past, pirates and other invaders discouraged the growth of tranquil fishing villages, but today the many natural harbours provide havens for new resorts and moorage for sailboats and yachts.

Just as varied are the landscapes of the interior. Over on the northwest side of the island, fertile foothills rise to the barren peaks of the Serra de Tramuntana. The terracing is attractively banked with dry-stone walling to hold in the soil for the olive groves and oak trees. The classical Mediterranean terrain of the lower hillsides is covered with heather and sweet-smelling rosemary, lavender and asphodel. Higher up, lichen is all that can survive. The tallest of the mountain peaks is Puig Major de Torella, 1,445 m (4,740 ft). Along with the Massanella and Tomir to the east, it is the home of rare black vultures, falcons and a nimble assortment of mountain goats.

The mountains erect a spectacular barrier to the formidable *tramuntana,* the northerly winds that give the range its name. But enough wind gets through to activate the mills scattered across the fertile plain. They pump the waters of Majorca's rich network of underground springs to irrigate the flatlands known as Es Pla. Here, the farmers rear cattle, pigs, sheep and horses and grow fruit, olives and almonds, cereals and flax for linen. Thanks to the fresh produce, you will find many of the best restaurants in the inland towns, notably at Inca and Binissalem.

The Little One

Minorca is quite simply smaller and quieter. With a total area of 702 sq km (271 sq miles), it is a fifth of the size of Majorca and has less than a tenth of the big sister's population. Nobody's complaining. British occupation in the 18th century seems to have left its mark not only on the colonial style of many houses but also on the genteel manners of the people. Even the island's rolling green countryside would be reminiscent of meadows in Sussex or Kent if it were not for rows of pumpkins ripening on the drystone walls. The magic crystalline light is Minorca's very own. The sometimes fierce *tramuntana* bends trees and bushes in fanciful, phantom-like shapes—olive, pine, and juniper, from which the British taught Minorcans to distil the gin for their favourite sunset tipple.

Mahón is a pleasant town, laid back from the open sea by a magnificent sheltered harbour which prompted the British to make it the island capital. At the other, western end of the island, Ciutadella was the original capital of the Church and aristocracy. It has retained a more traditional Mediterranean look with its arcades and the buff or ochre stone façades of Renaissance-style houses. Around town and along the south coast are several white sandy beaches, often in coves such as Cala Macarella and Cala Turqueta. Northern Minorca has only a few navigable natural harbours, notably Fornells. The adventure along this rocky coast is to explore the caves in the cliffs.

Flashback

Scenes From History

The anthropologists' meagre findings of significant bones and stones set the earliest human presence at around 5000 BC—hunters of a primitive form of antelope. Over the next few thousand years, the islands were settled, possibly by Iberians from North Africa (who later gave their name to the Spanish and Portuguese peninsula), intermarrying with Celts arriving from northern Europe. The true origin of these early settlers is hazy.

For their cereal farming and cattle grazing, the settlers had to clear away an amazing abundance of stones. The raw material made admirable houses, sanctuaries, fortifications, land boundaries and tall wind-breaker walls.

But these stones also proved very handy missiles. The islands' slingshot aces *(honderos)* won a formidable reputation throughout the western Mediterranean. They signed on as mercenaries to the Phoenicians and Greeks, the latter perhaps bequeathing the name "Balearic" from their verb *ballein*, "to throw". The Carthaginians, a Phoenician colony in what is now Tunisia, first invaded the islands in the 6th century BC. Settlements included the Minorcan towns of Jamna (Ciutadella) and Maghen (Mahón).

Romans and Barbarians

The great Carthaginian general Hannibal took Balearic *honderos* on his Italian campaign against the Romans in 218 BC. After Rome destroyed Carthage in the next century, the islands held out for 20 years. But in 123 BC, with thick sheets of ox hides protecting their ships against the Balearic ballistics, the soldiers of Quintus Caecilius Metellus overran the two islands they called *Balearis Major* and *Minor*.

The new colonization created an economic boom, with a strong garrison to fend off the ever-present threat of Mediterranean pirates. In Majorca, the Romans embarked on a classical building programme of roads and aqueducts and founded the towns of Palmaria (Palma) and Pollentia (Alcúdia). These ports traded in metals, textiles, much-valued ochre dye, glassware, ceramics, as well as slaves in transit. On Minorca, Mahón developed as a city of Jewish merchants and

Talatí de Dalt is one of Minorca's most attractive prehistoric sites.

FLASHBACK

artisans brought from Palestine following the destruction of Jerusalem in AD 70. And Latin laid the basis of the islands' version of the Catalan language.

In the 4th and 5th centuries, Vandals and Visigoths conquered the Romans on the Iberian peninsula and crossed over to the islands. They brought with them a particularly muscular form of Christianity, practising forced conversions on the pagans and massacring the recalcitrant Jews of Mahón in 418. A Byzantine fleet in turn drove the Vandals from the Balearics in 534. The islands became easy prey for pirates who left the towns in ruins.

Muslim Rule

The Moors, North Africans of Arab and Berber stock newly converted to Islam, crossed the Strait of Gibraltar in 711 and swept through Spain over the next ten years. Content to collect an annual tribute, they left the Balearic Islands in peace until payments stopped coming in the 9th century. The islands were duly occupied and annexed by the Caliphate of Cordoba in 902. Islamic religion and scholarship brought a new order and refinement to the anarchy left by centuries of brigandry. The Arabs appreciated the islands' pastures for their horses, cattle, sheep and goats and revived the culture of flax for linen, cereals and oil.

By the 11th century, renewed prosperity had once more made the islands a target for raiders from North Africa and the Spanish mainland. In 1127, Majorca organized itself as a separate and independent Arab kingdom.

Little has remained of the Muslims' monuments—a few Moorish arches, ornate palace gardens or the old bath-house in Palma, classical ceramics in

---

STONES, STONES, STONES

Stones small, big and gigantic are a distinctive feature of the Minorcan landscape. Farmers of old built up walls at the edge of their fields, ever taller until some country lanes became narrow stone corridors. The island is famous for its mysterious *talaiots* and *navetas*, respectively domed and elongated two-storey stone buildings, and for megalithic *taulas*, most often two slabs stacked one on top of the other to form a T. There are hundreds of these prehistoric structures scattered across Minorca, and no one knows for sure what they are. The best estimates date most of them between 2000 and 1300 BC. They may have been religious shrines, houses, fortifications or burial places.

the museums—but several Arab place-names still attest to their presence: Binissalem, Binisaïd, Alcúdia. More subtly, the cumin, cinnamon, pine nuts and almonds used in Majorcan cooking are unmistakably Moorish in inspiration. And few on Minorca would claim that later British contributions to local cuisine have managed to displace the Arabs' *alcuzcuz,* known locally as *cuscusso.*

The Reconquest

From the 10th century, Christian enclaves on the Spanish mainland began forming alliances to reconquer the peninsula over a period of 500 years. They regarded the Balearics as mere pirate strongholds in which the ports served as launching pads for Moorish raids on treasure ships. As his part of the spoils, Jaime I of Aragon seized Majorca in 1229 with 150 ships bearing a Christian army of 16,000 men and 1,500 horses. Finding fewer pirates than expected, the new Christian kingdom was at first happy to profit from the administrative services of the Moors and the island's Genoese and Jewish merchants. Muslim Minorca bought off immediate attack with an annual tribute of wheat and cattle, but in 1287, Alfonso III of Aragon trumped up a charge of treason to conquer and plunder the island, selling the Moors into slavery. Dynastic struggles among the Christian kings ended in Majorca being annexed to mainland Aragon in 1349.

With the Moors retrenched in their last mainland bastion of Granada, Christian rule did not bring peace to the islands. As if renewed piracy at sea, banditry on dry land, brutally repressed peasant rebellion and persecution of the Jews were not enough, a wave of famine and plague struck.

MINORCA'S ADMIRAL

To give him his full name, David Glasgow Farragut (1801–1870) must have learned a few things from the Ciutadella side of his family as he started his sailing career in time-honoured Minorcan fashion, fighting pirates—in the Gulf of Mexico and the Caribbean. In the American Civil War, despite his Southerner origins, he sided with the North's Union cause and was the US Navy's outstanding commander, both in seamanship and courage. He became the first American to achieve the rank of admiral after forcing the South's formidable defences in Mobile Bay with the now legendary cry: "Damn the torpedoes!"

FLASHBACK

When Palma was Christianized, the cathedral was erected on the site of the principal mosque, the Moorish Almudaina fortress was converted into a Gothic palace and the main synagogue became the Jesuit church, Església Monti-Sion. After the conquest of Granada by Queen Isabella of Castile and King Ferdinand of Aragon in 1492, the islands offered plenty of recruits for the ships—Spanish, French and British—that followed Columbus's route to America. In great demand were the Jews of Palma who had developed a special skill in map making.

Here Come the British

A Turkish army of 15,000 attacked Minorca in 1558, leaving Ciutadella in ruins and carrying most of its citizens off into captivity in Constantinople. The Majorcan ports of Alcúdia, Pollença and Sóller moved their townships inland. In 1615 and again in 1652, bubonic plague devastated the populace. By the beginning of the 18th century, the Balearic archipelago was little more than a strategic pawn in the struggles of the European Powers. Britain's alliance with the Austrian Habsburgs against the French Bourbons in the War of the Spanish Succession (1702–13) resulted in Britain getting Minorca (and Gibraltar), while the French took Majorca.

Though the Bourbons left little mark on the island, the British presence on Minorca can be felt to this day. After its capture in 1708, Minorca changed hands five times over the next century —falling to the French in 1756, retrieved by the British in 1763, succumbing to an eight-month

KEEPING THE FAITH

In the closed island society of Majorca, the Spanish Inquisition against Muslims and Jews was particularly virulent. The first trials began in 1232. In the two centuries after the Holy Office began its full-scale Inquisition in 1488, hundreds chose death rather than convert to Christianity. Many converts, Muslim *Moriscos* or Jewish *Xuetes* (Majorca's equivalent of the equally pejorative mainland term of *Marranos*), continued to practise their faith in secret. While most Muslims crossed to North Africa, clandestine Jews observed the Sabbath with a few words of remembered Hebrew. Their descendants still exercise the community's ancient skills as craftsmen and jewellers in Palma's old ghetto around Mount Zion Street.

Franco-Spanish siege in 1781 and reconquered a last time by the British in 1798 before being finally returned to the Spanish in 1802.

The first British governor, Richard Kane, began by making the port city of Mahón the capital of Minorca in place of Ciutadella, bastion of the Catholic church and the ultra-conservative aristocracy. Reinstating Minorca's old legal code, Kane ended the Inquisition, built new roads, introduced the cultivation of apples and showed the islanders how to turn juniper berries into gin.

Turbulent Times

Coup d'état, rebellion and war were the order of the day in 19th-century Spain as constitutional monarchy and regional republics staked their rival claims. Many islanders chose to emigrate—to the Black Sea, to Algeria or to Florida. One Minorcan family made it to Tennessee and produced the greatest naval hero of the American Civil War, Admiral David Farragut. Defying the turbulence, composer Frédéric Chopin and French novelist George Sand (male pseudonym of a betrousered baroness) carried on their liaison in a Majorcan monastery. Spain's overseas empire crumbled in Cuba, Puerto Rico and the Philippines. After the loss of Morocco in 1921, the dictatorship of General Primo de Rivera brought a semblance of law and order.

Civil War

The Spanish Republic of 1931 was born amid strikes, terrorist arson and violent street battles. Five years later, when General Francisco Franco led the revolt against the Republic, Majorca became a stronghold for the nationalist forces of monarchy, army, church and fascist Falange, while Minorca, always more sympathetic to the Catalan cause of nearby Barcelona, sided with the republican Popular Front of liberals, socialists, communists and anarchists.

From July 1936 to March 1937, 3,000 Republican loyalists were executed in Majorca. The church insisted that those to be

> **TALK OF THE ISLANDS**
>
> A national language, it is said, is a dialect with an army. This was particularly true of Castilian Spanish. At the end of the Civil War in 1939, the regime of General Franco suppressed the use of regional languages. With the restoration of democracy in 1975, Catalan came back into the open. The local dialects are known as Mallorquí and Menorquí.

killed be allowed to confess first, with a priest reporting in Palma: "Only 10 per cent of these dear children refused the last sacraments before being despatched by our good officers."

An invasion to reconquer Majorca with Republican troops from Catalonia and Valencia was repelled with the help of a squadron of Italian bomber pilots calling themselves "the Dragons of Death". Their red-bearded leader Arconovaldo Bonaccorsi, known as the Conte Rossi, became virtual dictator of Majorca. In black Fascist uniform with a white cross, he sped around the island in a red sports car, accompanied by an armed chaplain of the Spanish Falange to supervise the executions of Republicans.

Republican forces within the army on Minorca stopped the nationalist uprising in Mahón. General José Bosch and 11 senior officers were executed for high treason. Proud last stronghold of Republican resistance, the island capitulated only after the fall of Barcelona, in February 1939. The British navy was once more present. The captain of HMS *Devonshire* helped negotiate the island's surrender and shipped 450 Republican fighters to safety (for the time being) in Marseille.

Fascism then Democracy
Spain stayed out of World War II. Franco's dictatorship imposed the Spanish language and culture on the Balearic Islands. But the first waves of tourism in the 1950s opened the region to the outside world.

After Franco's death in 1975, the constitutional monarchy of Juan Carlos I guaranteed parliamentary democracy under which regional autonomy was negotiated for the Balearics. Priority was given to the local Mallorquí and Menorquí dialects. The islands profited by the tourist boom, particularly after Spain joined the European Community in 1986. Recent efforts aim at limiting expansion in favour of reviving traditional culture.

1

THE BEST CASTLE Only ruins remain of the islands' Moorish strongholds, but Palma's **Bellver Castle** is one of the most impressive medieval fortresses in all of Spain. The massive round edifice now houses a museum of the island capital's history, and its rooftop guard-walk provides a magnificent view of Majorca's mountains.

On the Scene

Whichever resort you choose as your base, each island is small enough for you to get to any of the sightseeing destinations and back again on the same day. With an early morning start, even an excursion to the other island can be a comfortable day trip. You just have to choose between the lively bounce of Majorca and the quieter life on Minorca.

▶ MAJORCA
Palma, Bay of Palma, West Coast, The Northwest, Northeast Coast, East Coast, South Coast, The Centre

The island's highways all lead (eventually) to or from Palma. And so, wherever you're staying, the island's capital is where we start.

Palma de Mallorca
Continuing the ancient tradition whereby the capital was known to its inhabitants just as "the city" (*Medina* to the Arabs), Majorcans refer to Palma as *Ciutat*. The current population of more than 390,000 accounts for half the island's permanent residents. This gives the port a big-city atmosphere not so very different from that of any major town on the mainland. But its earnest activities of regional government, commerce, textiles and the furniture industry combine with the more leisurely ambience of a Mediterranean resort. Its grand castle and the cathedral, churches and museum of the historic quarter attract the tourists by day, but later, the people of Palma reclaim their town for shopping and the institutional evening stroll, the *paseo*, on the broad avenues and boulevards.

The Port
Before plunging into the bustle of the town, take quiet stock of it down among the bobbing masts of the yachts and fishing boats in the harbour.

It wasn't always so peaceful. For the Romans, Moors and first Spanish conquerors, this was the hub of Palma's existence. In the shipyards, the Moors built a fleet

PALMA DE MALLORCA

of 100 vessels to battle with the ships of the Byzantine navy and the Spanish mainland. To the Venetians, Genoese and Turks, trade and contraband were indistinguishable in the port's traffic of gold, sugar, cotton and slaves. Islanders modestly contributed a little commerce in local honey and figs, wine and oil.

Today, the busiest folk are the menders of fishing nets, an activity as endless as the repainting of San Francisco's Golden Gate Bridge, along with a few desultory quayside anglers. (To get the best of the local fish, red mullet, you have to take a boat out to deeper waters.)

Cathedral

In *La Seu,* the city possesses one of Spain's great Gothic cathedrals. The limestone changes in colour throughout the day, from a cool buff in the morning and almost white at noon to a rich gold at sunset. It achieves the grace and strength of church and fortress with a phalanx of flying buttresses supporting the nave's massive core, topped by elegant spires.

Begun in 1230 on the site of the Moors' Great Mosque, the cathedral, with its forceful monumentality, made a clear statement to the rest of the Mediterranean world that Christianity had replaced Islam.

The Gothic portal facing the sea, the Mirador, is decorated with the 14th-century sculpture of Guillem Sagrera, depicting the *Last Supper.* On the western façade, the Renaissance portal was completed in 1601.

Inside, the light from rose windows at each end and stained glass in the aisles makes the lofty groin-vaulted nave appear much brighter than in most Spanish churches, since the choir structure was removed in 1904. This was the work of Catalan artist Antoni Gaudí (1852–1926), who designed the wrought-iron crown of thorns and canopy over the high altar and sculpture for the Royal Chapel *(Capilla Real),* inspired by his father, who was a coppersmith.

Museu Diocesà

In a building adjoining the Bishop's Palace *(Palau Episcopal)* just east of the cathedral, the museum has some medieval church painting and good examples of Moorish ceramics rescued from the mosque.

Almudaina Palace

Immediately west of the cathedral, the principal fortress of the Moorish governors was transformed into a predominantly Gothic edifice in the 13th century, and underwent extensive restoration in 1884. The guided visit

PALMA DE MALLORCA

includes the grand Council Room where King Juan Carlos convenes a ceremonial assembly of the Balearic Islands' regional government once a year. His royal apartments are closed to the public, as are the headquarters of the region's military garrison. The 14th-century Sant Ana chapel is used for the officers' Mass.

Royal Garden
Occasionally, the Spaniards knew a good Arab thing when they saw it. With its fountains playing among palm trees and rose bushes, cypress, juniper and eucalyptus, *S'Hort del Rei*—the King's Garden—recaptures the Arabs' genius for creating havens of cool tranquillity in the heat of the city. Modern taste has added sculpture by Alexander Calder and Joan Miró.

Curving gracefully across a pool with majestic black swans, the Arc de la Drassana Musulmana dates back to the 12th century when it was the gateway to the Moorish shipyards (before the waterfront receded to its present position).

Sa Llotja
Directly overlooking the main harbour, the old stock exchange (known in Spanish as *La Lonja*) is considered one of Spain's prime pieces of Gothic secular architecture. The sober 15th-century design of Guillem Sagrera has the simplest of decoration—corner turrets flanking the Gothic-arched main entrance and an open-work crennellated roof. Nowadays the building is noted for its remarkable temporary art exhibitions.

THE TWO BEST VIEWS One from down below, and one from up above. On Majorca, the most bewitching view of the cathedral's splendid Gothic spires, framed by the waterfront palm trees and the towers of the Llotja stock exchange, is from down below, on one of the jetties at the **Port of Palma**. Minorca has only one "mountain", **Monte Toro** appearing from the air scarcely more than a molehill, but neatly placed in the middle of the island's rolling plain. From the top, you can see the north and south coasts and the lovely patchwork of the stone-walled meadows.

PALMA DE MALLORCA

Consolat de Mar
Next to the stock exchange, what was in the 17th century the maritime courthouse now serves as the seat of the Balearic Islands' regional government. The largely Renaissance structure also houses a small Naval Museum.

Es Baluard
On Plaça Porta de Santa Catalina, the old bastion of Sant Pere now houses a gallery of modern and contemporary art, displaying a vast collection of paintings, sculpture, drawings and ceramics from the end of the 19th century to the present. It includes works by Picasso, Gauguin, Cézanne, Miro, Giacometti, Magritte and Picabia, along with other artists with Balearic connections, such as Santiago Rusiñol.

Avinguda del Rei Jaume III
Cutting across the town, this bustling shopping street in the neoclassical style of the late 19th century groups fashionable boutiques, travel agencies, banks and the more traditional hotels.

Es Born
This stately tree-lined thoroughfare is the major focus of that grand Mediterranean institution the *paseo*, the evening promenade. From the open-air cafés and public benches, spectators watch several generations of smartly dressed families parading up and down, taking the air. The boulevard coming down from the city centre at Plaça Rei Joan Carles I to the Plaça de la Reina follows the old riverbed of the Torrent de la Riera which provided a natural moat for the original Moorish fortifications. After the river was diverted to the west (to Passeig Mallorca), Es Born was at first an arena for jousting tournaments.

Ajuntament
The town hall on Plaça Cort is a suitably august edifice of Renaissance and baroque design (1680) with a long upper balcony from which the town's elders can salute an appreciative electorate.

Patrician Mansions
Palma's Spanish nobility built their homes east of the cathedral in the Portella neighbourhood laid out by the Moors. Many of the larger houses were built 400 years ago and embellished in the 18th century in an Italian Renaissance or baroque style. Beyond the limestone façades, through the doorways' iron grilles, you will catch glimpses of ornate balconied courtyards with graceful arcades and monumental staircases. Among the best examples are Can Oleza on Carrer Morey, Can Oleo on Carrer Almudaina and Palau Vivot, with Corinthian columns, on Carrer Savellà.

PALMA DE MALLORCA

Museu de Mallorca
Majorca's principal museum, in the old Desbrull Palace, displays Roman, Moorish and Gothic Christian art from around the island. The collection includes Palma church paintings from the 13th to 15th centuries and works of modern Majorcan artists.

Banys Àrabs
Signposted through the maze of streets, the 11th-century Arab Baths on Carrer Serra are a last vestige of Moorish life in the medina. Step into the old garden and another world of orange trees and palms, of Islamic horseshoe arches. In the bath house is the "hot room" for steam baths and a cooling-off room with openings in its roof and tapering columns each with a different ornate capital.

Es Call
East of Portella, the old neighbourhood of the Jewish merchants, jewellers and craftsmen was located around Carrer Monti-Sion and Seminari. The jewellery shops and workshops are still there, run by descendants of those who, after the expulsions of 1492, stayed behind either as clandestinely practising Jews or as converted Christians. One of the two synagogues is now a Jesuit church, Església MontiSion. Its baroque façade is adorned with statues of saints Ignatius of Loyola and Francis Xavier flanking the order's coat of arms beneath the figure of Mary. The other synagogue was transformed into a Catholic seminary.

Basílica de Sant Francesc
Construction of the monastery church began in 1281. American visitors in particular will be interested in the square's statue of Majorca-born Junípero Serra (1713–84), doughty Franciscan founder of Californian missions from San Diego to Monterey. A 17th-century baroque façade contrasts with the dark but imposing groin-vaulted Gothic interior. In the apse is the tomb of Palma's illustrious 13th-century theologian and scholar Ramón Llull. Rest a while in the monastery's broad square cloister, still a popular focus of communal activity.

Plaça Major
From here to the town hall is the pedestrian zone of the popular marble-paved shopping district. The square itself attracts a colourful crowd, day and night. Over on its west side, facing La Rambla, is the town theatre, *Teatre Principal,* noted for its classical music concerts and recitals.

Castell de Bellver
On the west side of town, this superb medieval castle is, as a landmark, a worthy rival to the

PALMA DE MALLORCA

Miró's works are much appreciated by modern Majorcans.

cathedral. It rises above a grand hillside park of pine trees that is a favourite with Palma's joggers. Bellver's unusual three-tiered circular design combines a massive exterior with a slender-columned Gothic arcade surrounding the inner courtyard. It served as fortress and palace. There is a dazzling view from the roof over Palma's bay and across to the northern mountains. Once a dungeon for prisoners of the Inquisition and Franco's dictatorship, the castle is now a well-arranged Museum of Municipal History from prehistoric through Roman, Moorish and feudal Christian times.

Joan Miró Foundation

This striking modern museum devoted to the works of the celebrated painter has been built on the site of his studios, on Palma's western outskirts at Cala Major. The handsome structures make a deliberate, almost provocative contrast with the surrounding uninspired apartment blocks and hotels. Miró, whose mother was born in Majorca, lived on the island from 1940. (It must be said that Majorcans did not begin to appreciate his art until after his death, in 1983.)

The colourful collections include more than 100 of Miró's oil paintings, mainly from the 1960s and 70s, as well as hundreds of drawings and prints, and his personal collection of modern Spanish artists, Saura and Tapiès, together with other contemporaries such as Calder, Chagall and Adami.

Bay of Palma

The bay describes a curve of 40 km (25 miles) from S'Arenal and Les Meravelles on the east around to Palma Nova and Magalluf on the west. The long stretches of finest white sand on beaches sloping gently into the sea for shallow bathing make it ideal for families. The bay's western headland is more craggy, marked by the rocky creeks and caves of Portals Vells—a haven for nudists.

S'Arenal-Les Meravelles

This exuberant twin resort complex boasts one of the longest family beaches on the bay. For much of the seafront, the incline is so gradual that the Mediterranean seems like a wading pool for splashing youngsters. In addition to a first-class swimming pool, the Arenal Sport Centre has facilities for tennis, squash, minigolf, bowling and badminton. You can go horseback riding at Picadero Son Sunyer riding school, or sailing at Arenal's Club Náutico and in the neighbouring harbour of Ca'n Pastilla.

On the main highway from Palma to S'Arenal, Aquacity is a huge aquatic fun park featuring a seemingly endless spiral waterchute. The resort is also renowned for its nightlife ranging from discos to Bavarian-style beer gardens.

In a region particularly popular with German-speaking visitors, Sunday mass is held in German at a couple of local churches. Another church, in Les Meravelles, conducts Sunday mass in English and French in addition to German.

Illetes

The beaches of Illetes are beautifully framed by pine woods and bizarre rock formations. Among the illustrious figures who frequented the region, Errol Flynn, the man who as Robin Hood stole the hearts of the rich *and* of the poor, or at least their young daughters, is commemorated with a plaque beside the Hotel Albatros.

Portals Nous

This quieter resort is appreciated for its elegant villas enjoying easy access to a pine-shaded sandy cove. Its name, "New Arches", refers to the caves—ancient, in fact—in the rocks near the sea. Yachting facilities have been developed at the new marina of Porto Portals.

BAY OF PALMA • WEST COAST

Looming over the local golf course is the restored castle of Bendinat, where King Jaime I stopped for a meal that consisted only of a few chunks of garlic bread after fighting his way inland from Santa Ponça in his invasion of Reconquest in 1229.

The star attraction for families here is the dolphin show at the Marineland in neighbouring Costa d'en Blanes.

Magalluf
The beaches in this popular resort are set amid spectacular coves of pines and palm trees. There is someone for everyone here, with a wealth of water sports, starting with windsurfing, water-skiing, paragliding and sailing. Kids work off excess energy at an exciting aqua park and Wild West theme park. Nightlife is highlighted by cabarets, flamenco dancing, discos, and a casino at Cala Xada with a floor-show to warm up the clients for the gambling tables.

West Coast
To the west of the Bay of Palma, the coast becomes steadily more craggy. Long beaches give way to romantic coves, sheer cliffs and rocky outcrops. Sailing, surfing and scuba diving come into their own, but there are a few stretches of sand for family bathing, too.

WEST COAST

Santa Ponça
The popular seaside resort is the spot where King Jaime I of Aragon landed with his infantry and cavalry on September 10, 1229 to capture the island from the Moors. In those days, it was a marshy wilderness. The historic site, on the Sa Caleta promontory near the yacht club, is marked by a monumental stone cross erected on the 700th anniversary, with scenes of the conquest carved in bas-relief. Today's invaders are more peaceable, paragliding or windsurfing across the bay.

Peguera and Cala Fornells
The swimming and other water sports here benefit from the cooling shelter of pine woods and the mountain country behind. Hiking into the Serra Garrafa hills makes a refreshing change from the beach.

Port d'Andratx
Like many a coastal town, Andratx was for centuries an attractive target for Turkish pirates, and finally the bulk of its community moved inland. The old port is today a pleasant resort with a yachting harbour.

Andratx
For a change of pace, head inland to explore the maze of the little town of Andratx itself. On the northern edge of town is the 16th-century Tower of San Mas which, in the absence of the local military commander, was valiantly defended against the pirates by his wet-nurse. Her victory is depicted in a painting in the parish church.

South of town on the road to Capdella, the Centro Cultural Andratx comprises two exhibition spaces for modern art, the Kunsthalle and Asbaek Gallery. Built in traditional Majorcan style around a colonnaded patio, the centre is set in beautiful natural surroundings, with its own spring and natural pool.

Sant Telm
Named after the sailors' patron saint Erasmus or Elmo, a 4th-century martyr, the port grew up around a sailors' hospital and oratory built by King Jaime II in 1279. After Arab attack, the building was transformed into the fortress visible today. A few fishermen hang on, recalling with nostalgia the smuggling days of their fathers in the 1940s.

Illa de Dragonera
Just west of Sant Telm, beyond the tiny isle of Pantaleu, is the island of Dragonera, a granite hill rising to 310 m (over 1000 ft) above sea level. It has recently been declared a nature reserve for a rare species of lizard, successfully defended against tourist

WEST COAST • THE NORTHWEST

development and now having to cope only with the island's equally uncommon species of falcons and gulls.

The Northwest

The island's most spectacular landscapes are to be found after the road cutting north from Andratx reaches the coast, where Majorca's principal mountain range, the Serra de Tramuntana, spills down into the Mediterranean. Since Moorish times, farmers have sought to "hold back" the precipitation by banking the meagre soil with stone walls. The result is an enchanting pattern of terraces for the crops of cereals and vegetables and groves of olives and orange trees. To protect their property against marauding pirates, they also built an early-warning system of lookout towers along the coast, several still standing.

Estallencs and Banyalbufar

The two farming villages are set back from the coast, flanked by terraced fields with pine woods rising behind them. In each case, their little fishing ports and a rocky cove for swimming can be reached by narrow winding roads best tackled on foot. You'll get a great view of the coast from the lookout towers on either side of Estallencs: Mirador de Ricard Roca and spiral-staircased Mirador de Ses Animes.

La Granja

This old feudal farming estate is a short drive inland from Banyalbufar, northeast along the Esporles road. Originally owned by Moors, it has since belonged variously to an Aragonese count, Cistercian monks, Spanish gentlemen farmers and

---

> **GEORGE AND FRED**
>
> "Monkeys," she said of the islanders, going on to describe them as thieves and barbarians. Their feeling for the celebrated French novelist who called herself George Sand was decidedly mutual. They didn't like this haughty divorcee wearing men's clothes and smoking cigars, and who didn't go to church. By her own account, the lady born Aurore Dupin spent a wretched two months in the charterhouse of Valldemossa with her lover, Frédéric Chopin. The Polish composer was racked by a lung disease, and his own piano was delayed at customs until a few days before they were due to leave. At any rate, she got a book out of it, *A Winter in Majorca* and, on an instrument borrowed locally, he created some of his best pieces for solo piano.

now Majorcan entrepreneurs who have transformed it into a picturesque living and working craft museum. Country folk in traditional costume can be seen spinning wool, making pottery, jewellery, lace and embroidery, weaving linen and carpets. They also bake pastries and fig bread, which can be tasted here, along with the local sweet wines and orange or lemon liqueurs. The mansion is in part furnished in the 18th-century styles of Spain, France and Italy. Most pleasant of all are the farm's gardens, the gushing natural springs and the surrounding woods.

Valldemossa

Spread across a valley in the Serra de Tramuntana, the town has a quaint charm that would make it worth the trip even without the fame of its ardent 19th-century visitors, composer Frédéric Chopin, author George Sand, and her children Maurice and Solange.

The neat little houses are decorated with flowers and ceramic tiles honouring Catalina Thomàs, the island's patron saint, born in Valldemossa. The town celebrates the saint's day in the last week of July, with music accompanying Catalina's carriage in a costumed procession. The house where she was born in 1533 is now a chapel adjoining the parish church of San Bartomeu. The church's 18th-century belfry looks across the valley to the similar late-baroque tower of the celebrated Carthusian monastery, Sa Cartuja *(Sa Cartoixa)*.

Sa Cartuja

The monastery acquired by Carthusian monks in 1339 was progressively transformed and rebuilt over the centuries until the

---

THE THREE BEST MONASTERIES After the Reconquista, thanks to the Christians' missionary zeal, the monasteries of Majorca became centres not only of study and devotion for monks but also of pilgrimage for the islanders. This is still true today for the **Convent Sant Francesc** in Palma and **Lluc Monastery** in the Tramuntana mountains. The third, Valldemossa's **Sa Cartuja**, has been secularized but still attracts the equally fervent pilgrimage of tourists drawn by the saga of George Sand and Frédéric Chopin.

THE NORTHWEST

order was expelled by the Spanish government in 1835. In its beautiful mountain setting, it became a very comfortable boarding house with cells converted into cosy apartments looking out onto the monastery gardens—including a maze—and 16th-century cloister. The rooms occupied by George Sand and Frédéric Chopin in 1838 have become a museum with personal effects, original manuscripts and two pianos used by the composer. Subsequent artist-boarders included the great Latin American writers Rubén Darío and Jorge Luis Borges—who studied Latin with the curate of Valldemossa. The church is largely an 18th-century structure replacing the original Gothic one built in 1445. A pharmacy has been reconstituted to evoke the shop where the brothers concocted their medicines. Included in the monastery buildings is a once royal palace, the Palau del Rei Sanç.

Costa Nord de Valldemossa

At Avenida Palma 6, this cultural centre, partly financed by actor Michael Douglas, hosts concerts and temporary exhibitions highlighting the area's natural beauty and heritage.

Son Marroig

Magnificently located just off the coast road west of Deià, the estate that belonged to the 19th-century Austrian amateur naturalist, Habsburg Archduke Ludwig Salvator (*Luis Salvador* to Majorcans), is now open to the public. Visit the opulently furnished clifftop mansion where he received his empress cousin Sissi, and enjoy the sweeping views of the coast from the upstairs terrace or down in the charming gardens. In summer, open-air concerts are held in the courtyard. A signposted path takes you down to the Na Foradada promontory with its formidable gaping hole which sea and wind have worn away. It was here that the archduke moored his yacht and where dauntless swimmers take a Spartan dip.

Deià

Popular with the showbiz children and grandchildren of the flower-children who gathered here in the 1960s, this village's buff-coloured houses hug the hillside around their fortress-like parish church. Up in the pretty little cemetery, a simple tomb bears the words *Robert Graves: Poeta,* to honour the great English writer who, long before the hippies, made Deià his home. He first lived here in the 1930s, writing *I, Claudius* and its sequel,

Deià is one of Majorca's most picturesque villages.

THE NORTHWEST

Claudius the God, until forced to flee the Spanish Civil War. He returned after World War II to write the bulk of his poetry, and died in 1985, aged 90. For a bracing swim, try the pebble beach at the fishing harbour of Cala de Deià.

Sóller

The most enjoyable journey to this town at the heart of the Serra de Tramuntana mountains is the train ride in posh wooden carriages covering the 36 km (22 miles) from Palma in 90 minutes. The views are enchanting as you pass through valleys of orange and lemon orchards and groves of olives and almonds—the latter with a bonus of glorious blossom in January and February. Sóller itself (in Arabic "Golden Valley") has a certain Gallic air to it, since many of its people emigrated to France in the 19th century and returned to build themselves mansions in French château style. The town comes to life in the evening in the cafés and restaurants around Plaça Constitució.

Fornalutx and Biniraix

These handsome villages clinging to the mountainside just east of Sóller are worth a visit for their characteristic Majorcan rural architecture. Many of the limestone houses have been lovingly restored—and a couple of open-air restaurants offer bewitching panoramas over the terraced valley.

Port de Sóller

An old-fashioned tram rolls down from Sóller on a delightful trip through the citrus orchards and along the seafront to the town's fishing port. In the 16th century, the harbour was the scene of many violent pirate assaults, one of them fought off with two sisters, Catalina and Francisca Casasnovas, leading the counterattack. The heroic battle of 1516 is annually re-enacted in May. Yachts and other sailing craft have joined the fishermen in what is now a pleasant resort with cafés and restaurants around the sandy bay.

Sa Calobra

Getting to this most spectacular of the island's coves—east along the coast from Port de Sóller—is an exploit. From the mountain highway at the Gorg Blau reservoir that supplies much of Palma's drinking water, the 13 km (8 miles) of bends leading to the sea are not just hairpins. They twist back on themselves in seemingly impossible double turns down, and giddily up and down again, before reaching Cala de Sa Calobra. The ride is "fun" enough in a car. On a bicycle, it is positively hallucinogenic. If you can keep your eyes open, grand mountain vistas unfold all along the way, with goats and sheep looking on in disbelief and an occasional fox in the hunting reserve, clearly smiling.

The smooth white pebble beach leads back through a tunnel eroded in the rocks, along the stunning canyon of the Pareis river. In the natural amphitheatre among the canyon's pools of fresh water, choral concerts are held in the first half of July. Sa Calobra has plenty of good seafood restaurants.

Lluc Monastery

Thanks to its isolated position high among the Tramuntana's densely wooded ravines, Lluc has been the site of religious worship since pagan prehistoric times. Today, it is the focus of the island's most revered pilgrimage.

The centre of veneration is the Black Virgin, *La Moreneta,* shrouded in legend. The devout date the sculpture back to the monastery's foundation in the 13th century, the time of the *Reconquista,* but some scholars think the statue may be even older, not originally Christian but possibly a representation of the Egyptian goddess, Isis. Over the centuries, Majorcans have donated pearls, emeralds and diamonds to embellish La Moreneta's double crown.

Some 900 m (nearly 3,000 ft) up in the mountains, the present monastery buildings are mostly 18th-century. Modern Catalan architect Antoni Gaudí designed

---

WALKING IN THE MOUNTAINS

Sóller is a popular base for ramblers who want to explore the Serra de Tramuntana. Before you venture off on foot, first call in at the local tourist office for trail-maps and helpful information. A favourite walk is the scenic route down to Deià. Just northeast of Sóller, the island's tallest mountain, Puig Major, 1,445 m (4,740 ft), is out of bounds to climbers because of the military radar on the summit. If you want to attempt the climb up Puig Massanella, 1,348 m (4,422 ft), further east, the local Sóller-Pollença bus will take you to the starting point (near the Lluc filling station) for an easy-going hike to the top and back in under 5 hours. Near the summit, there's a fresh-water spring, so you can foil the black vultures you may spot hovering around in search of lunch. But in any case, avoid the climb in high summer.

the fanciful monuments marking the Stations of the Cross that lead to the sanctuary.

A major attraction of the monastery is Mass sung by the blue-clad Es Blauets boys' choir. The Lluc museum exhibits local archaeological finds and a historic collection of church robes.

Alfàbia Mansion

Crossing the island from Palma to Sóller by road rather than train, you can stop and stroll through the grounds of this country manor from another age on the southern slopes of the Tramuntana mountains.

Since the 13th century, when it was the residence of the Moorish vizir of Palma, the house has gone through many transformations, Gothic, Renaissance and ultimately baroque. But there is still an undeniably Arabian atmosphere to the cool exotic gardens now left in romantic neglect.

Alaró Castle

Another excursion east of the Palma-Sóller road takes you through the village of Bunyola (with its noteworthy baroque church) on a lovely winding route towards the hilltop ruin of a venerable Moorish fortress. Once in the hands of the Spanish, it was the focus of violent battles between rival rulers of Aragon, leaving it in its present war-scarred condition. The last part of the journey to the flat summit of the Puig d'Alaró, at 822 m (2,696 ft) has to be tackled on foot, but the view makes it worthwhile.

Northeast Coast

The broad Bay of Pollença offers a privileged holiday destination with the combined attractions of fine white sands at its easy-going beach resorts and the wild rugged beauties of the Formentor peninsula's pine forests, rocky cliffs and sandy coves.

Pollença

The town takes its name from a Roman port, *Pollentia* (originally located close to present-day Alcúdia) but was in fact established only in 1230. It was founded inland by the Alcúdians to protect themselves from marauding pirates. The so-called Roman Bridge, a pretty twin-arched stone structure on the eastern outskirts of town, was most probably built by Vandal invaders in the 5th century. In the city centre, some stately limestone buildings date back to the heyday of the Knights of the Order of St John, who occupied Pollença in the 18th century.

Of the two hills flanking the town, the one on the west, Puig del Calvari, presents a formidable challenge. A flight of 365 stairs (which the most fervent climb on their knees) leads through a lovely avenue of cypresses up to the little 18th-century Calvary Chapel at the top. The reward is a splendid view over the town and across to the bays of Pollença and Alcúdia. Further south is the Santuari de Puig de Maria, a hilltop monastery which provides accommodation—and good food—for visitors.

Port de Pollença

The resort, 7 km (4 miles) from Pollença, has the most pleasant sandy beaches and an atmosphere much more relaxed than that prevailing in the boisterous resorts on the Bay of Palma. It also makes an excellent base for explorations into the Formentor peninsula, and the facilities for water sports are first class.

Formentor

Pointing like an outstretched finger into the Mediterranean, the craggy peninsula provides a nicely dramatic climax to the sweep of the Tramuntana mountains. Some of the cliffs plunge 200 m (656 ft) down to the sea, where secluded creeks and coves provide beaches from which to swim out to rocky outcrops and promontories.

You can take the winding road 20 km (12 miles) through the forest to the lighthouse at Cap de Formentor; alternatively, boats from resorts on the Bay of Pollença dock at the pine-shaded beaches of Cala Pi de la Posada, Cala Engossaubas and Platja de Formentor.

Even if you are not staying there, the sumptuous Hotel Formentor is a Majorcan institution at which you can take a peek—perhaps with a drink or meal on the terrace. It was built in the 1920s by a German-Argentinian who went bankrupt seven years after its inauguration. With its opulent park, the hotel has at-

4

THE FOUR BEST CAVES The cliffs are honeycombed with caves. The best-known on Majorca, bathed in light and music, are the **Coves del Drac** and **Coves dels Hams,** both on the east coast near Porto Cristo. Further north, with remarkable stalagmites and stalactites, are the **Coves de Artà.** On the south coast of Minorca, the most popular cave, **Cova d'en Xoroi** is now a bar and night club.

NORTHEAST COAST

tracted Europe's crowned heads and such Hollywood royalty as Charlie Chaplin, Peter Ustinov and Michael Douglas.

Alcúdia

This, not Pollença, is the original site of the ancient settlement founded by the Romans in the 2nd century BC as *Pollentia*. The imposing ramparts, erected in part by the Moors, have two monumental gates which were added in the 15th century, Porta de Xara on the east side and Porta Sant Sebastià on the west. The fortified church of Sant Jaume is built into the walls' southern bastion. A small archaeological museum in a handsome old building opposite exhibits Roman artefacts. More interesting, just south of town, is a Roman theatre.

S'Albufera Nature Reserve

On the road from Alcúdia to Ca'n Picafort, in the marshlands near the shores of Alcúdia Bay, ornithologists have counted more than 200 species of migrant and native birds. The sanctuary covers some 1,200 hectares (3,000 acres) and hosts bitterns, falcons, kingfishers, terns, plovers, lapwings, moorhens and other water fowl. You can rent binoculars at the reserve's reception centre.

Ca'n Picafort

At the heart of Alcúdia Bay, vast beaches and an endlessly energetic night life have made this one of the fastest growing resort towns on the island. About 10 km (6 miles) inland, Muro makes an interesting excursion for its bull-ring carved out of the rock and a first-rate ethnological museum assembling the island's prehistoric tools and utensils in an attractive mansion.

East Coast

Modern resort villages have mushroomed around the coast's sheltered coves and fishing harbours. The elements have drilled caves deep into the cliffs; exploring the subterranean waters is an adventure. The easterly breezes are right for windsurfing and sailing, the rocky coast perfect for diving and underwater photography, and there are sandy beaches to keep the lazier members of the family happy, too.

Porto Cristo

This stylish resort built around a sheltered harbour snaking deep inland makes an ideal base for exploring the region. The children enjoy the broad expanse of beach and an aquarium with piranhas and electric eels. Up on the cliff above the port are the ruins of an early Christian church, Sa Carroja, dating back to the 6th century. Before that, Porto Cristo was an important mooring for the Roman fleet. In the 20th century, it was the beachhead for the doomed Republican attempt to capture Majorca from Franco's rebels in 1936.

Coves del Drac

Barely 1 km (half a mile) south along the coast from Porto Cristo, the Dragon Caves count among the most popular attractions on the island. The crash of the roiling sea against the rocks is a fearsome spectacle, but the grottoes' illuminated underground lakes are hypnotically calm. Flat-bottomed boats take you along canals from one cave to the other past amazing patterns of stalagmites and stalactites, the whole eerily enhanced by the music of Chopin.

Coves dels Hams

Further inland, but also linked to the sea by underground rivers, the smaller Fish Hook Caves derive their name from their bizarrely hooked stalactites. The main underground lake is narrower than that of the Dragon, but the atmosphere is more enjoyably spooky.

Porto Colom

Residents of this pleasant little fishing village like to boast that Christopher Columbus got his name from ancestors living here.

East Coast

They might do better with the considerable achievement of having exported local wine to France in the 19th century—from the Felanitx vineyards.

The fishermen's neatly kept houses, as trim as their eternally repaired nets and repainted boats, give the harbour genuine charm.

Cala d'Or
This is one of the biggest, best-equipped resorts on the island. State-of-the-art facilities for water sports attract a vigorous array of divers, paragliders, water-skiers, windsurfers, deep-sea fishermen and yachtsmen.

The lighthouse at Porto Colom.

Cala Figuera
The brightly coloured houses make this beautifully sheltered Y-shaped fishing harbour one of the most attractive spots on the east coast. Relatively quiet bathing is available in the nearby secluded coves around the headland at Cala Santanyí and Cala Lombarts.

Artà
In the northeast, this quiet village retains a good part of its medieval ramparts below the hilltop fortress-church of Sant Salvador. Among the country squires' old mansions, a few artisans still practise the ancient craft of basketry, weaving hats, fans and chairs.

On the southern edge of town is Ses Païsses, the island's largest prehistoric settlement. It was built over a period of four centuries from 1200 BC. Parts of its outer fortifications still flank an imposing solid megalithic entrance. Inside is a complex of dwellings as well as a monumental *talaiot,* a large, circular, well-like structure sunk into a mound, believed to have served as a shrine or tomb.

Capdepera
On the eastern cape that bears its name, this hillside village nestles around the battlements of a 14th-century fortress. Walk along the ramparts to share the view the soldiers had of their invaders from the sea—these days, flotillas of windsurfers and water-skiers.

Cala Ratjada
The east coast's most popular holiday resort is favoured particularly by German tourists. The town's fishermen vie with the yachts for moorings in the old port. In the grounds of Sa Torre Cega, a country house, is a sculpture garden of works by Auguste Rodin, Henry Moore and Barbara Hepworth among modern Spanish masters. Guided tours are arranged by the tourist office.

Coves de Artà
Carved by the elements from the limestone cliffs of Cape Vermell, the caves (entrance at the top of a long flight of steps) have several cathedral-like halls where the stalagmites and stalactites have grown together to form pillars. They are linked by an intricate labyrinth of passages and stairways. One of the natural pillars measures 22 m (72 ft) in height and is still growing roofwards. The biggest of the caverns is the Hall of Flags, 45 m (147 ft) high.

In the lowest gallery, named after Dante's *Inferno,* a sound and light show is performed to the inspiring organ music of Johann Sebastian Bach.

South Coast
Remote from the main tourist centres, the beaches on the south

coast are wilder rolling sand dunes, providing seclusion for nudist bathing and sanctuaries for rare birds. It is also a region of prehistoric monuments.

Es Trenc
This is the beach area most appreciated by nudist swimmers. They are a peaceful flock, sharing the pine-shaded dunes with lizards and waterfowl. From the nearby harbour of Sant Jordi, birdwatchers can rent a small boat to go out to the little isle of Cabrera for the reserve's falcons, fish eagles, peregrines and cormorants. You may be accompanied by a dolphin or two.

Capocorp Vell
West of Es Trenc, some 5 km (3 miles) inland behind Cala Pi, is a prehistoric village of *talaiot* mounds and towers and megalithic *taulas*. Deployed on strategic positions overlooking the sea, the structures may have been fortified defences against pirates.

The Centre
Holidaymakers tend to neglect the interior, the plain or Es Pla between the Tramuntana mountains and the south and east coasts. But this is where the Majorcans get their work done, and there's a fair sprinkling of good restaurants off the tourists' beaten track.

Inca
The prosperous town of 30,000 inhabitants has made its fortune from leather. Seek out the old wine cellars where the Incans hide their best restaurants—the roast suckling pig and *longaniza* sausage are heavenly. You can pay a visit to the 14th-century Sant Francesc monastery, and sample the nuns' *concos* cakes at the Sant Jeroni Convent. The town is also reputed for its dark-hued pottery. Thursday is market day, one of the island's main weekly events.

Binissalem
The vineyards here produce some of the island's better wines. While you're here, you can try the local reds made from *mantonegro* and *callet* grapes. You'll be an expert when it comes to ordering wine on your nights out.

Felanitx
For centuries a centre of wine-bottling, the town is also renowned for its ceramics. The pottery workshops are open to the public. You can buy the ornate and nicely fashioned wine jugs— *gerres brodades* or the more robust *greixoneres* used for oven-baking.

In early spring, the interior bursts into clouds of almond blossom.

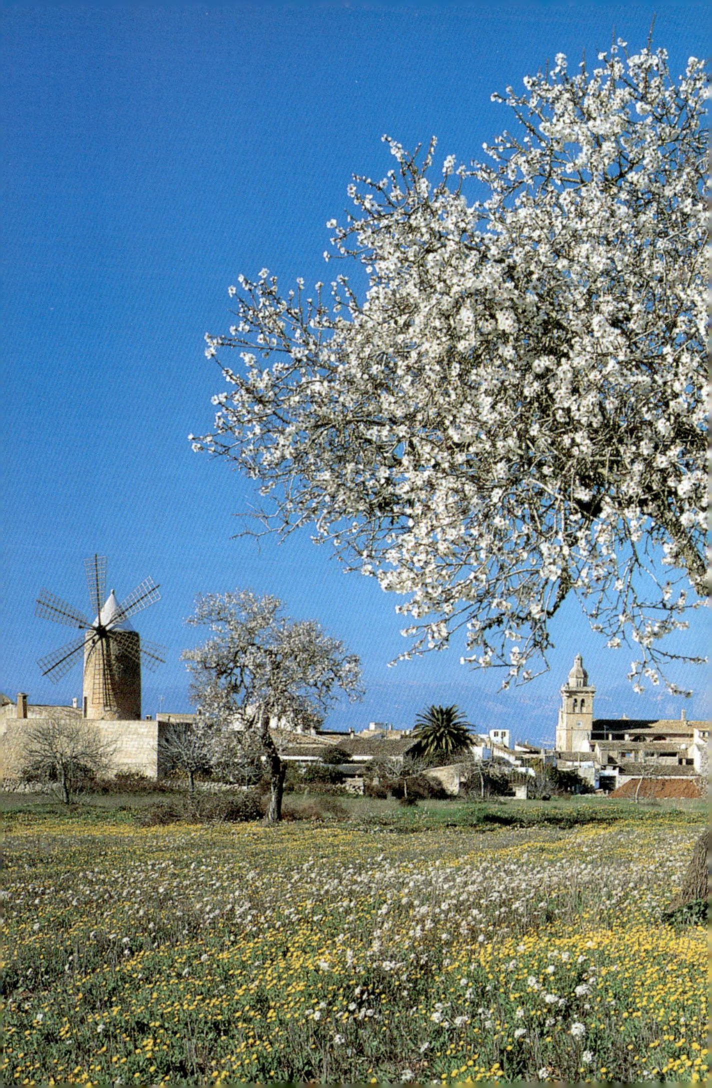

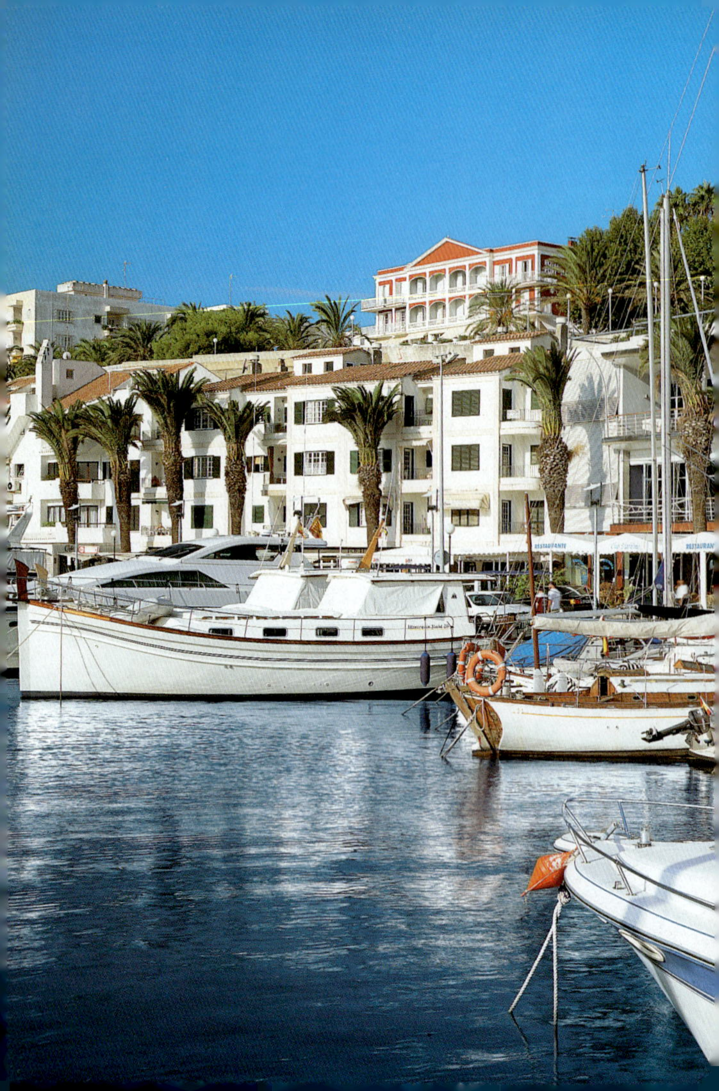
RESTAURANTE

MINORCA

Mahón, The Southeast, The North, The Centre, Ciutadella, Western Beaches

---

The island has had two capitals, the eastern port city of Mahón *(Maó)* replacing the old Spanish Christian and aristocratic bastion of Ciutadella at the western end. Both remain Minorca's major sightseeing attractions. They are 45 km (28 miles) apart, linked by a first-class highway. Most of the beach resorts are on the south coast. The famous prehistoric stone *talaiots* and *taulas* are scattered across the centre, a rolling plain with just one mountain, El Toro, rising in the middle.

Mahón

Since the ancient Phoenicians, Mediterranean navigators have sung the praises of this port sheltered from the open sea by its deep-water channel, over 5 km (3 miles) long. It has been cherished by Genoese merchant-cum-pirate Andrea Doria, Turkish pirate Barbarossa (born on the Greek island of Lesbos) and England's Admiral Nelson. Miraculously, unlike most great sea ports, it has remained spick and span, characterized by neatly painted Georgian houses with sash and bow windows bequeathed by the British, and a sprinkling of gleaming white Spanish houses to remind you of the present masters. The occasional Burgundy-hued façades are a throwback to the paint used in the shipyards to protect against rot and rust.

The Harbour

Stroll at random along the quays past boatyards, yacht clubs, ship's chandlers, fishermen unloading their catch or mending their nets, seafood restaurants and bars. Boats of all kinds tie up in the port, from pleasure craft to hard-working trawlers. You can tour one of the waterfront distilleries that have been producing gin since the British arrived in the 18th century. Some connoisseurs find the local product, decanted in earthenware carafes, to be the equal of the most celebrated British or Dutch brands. A distillery visit, including a gin-tasting session, may be included in the harbour cruises around the waterway's little islands. A cruise will give you a good view of the old fortresses on the promontories commanding the harbour mouth at La Mola and Punta de Sant Carles.

Mahón, an elegant town hemming the harbourside.

MAHÓN

The Market
An intricately winding road, Costa de ses Voltes, and staircases lead from the port up to the *Mercat,* the town's vegetable and fish market on Plaça del Carme. The colourful stalls are laid out along the arcades of an 18th-century Carmelite convent. This is a handy place to get to know the local cheeses, tough and tangy *curado* or soft and creamy *tierno.* Like any self-respecting market, it is surrounded by good cafés and bars for *tapas.*

Church of Santa Maria
After his conquest of the island, King Alfonso III of Aragon razed the town's principal mosque to make way for this Gothic edifice in 1287. It was rebuilt in the 18th century and is still the town's main church. The king's statue stands on the nearby Plaça de la Conquesta. The church's baroque ornament is undistinguished, but the interior is notable for the outsize wooden organ built in Barcelona in 1808 by the Swiss Johann Kyburz. With more than 3,000 pipes and four keyboards, it is considered one of the best organs in Europe. The church offers recitals most days in summer.

Ajuntament
On Plaça de la Constitució, the town hall was begun in 1613 and completed in Grecian classical style in 1788. An English touch is added to its wrought-iron balconies and Doric columns with the 18th-century clock donated by the island's first British governor, Richard Kane.

Carrer de Isabel II
This street leading northwest from the town hall has several

THE FIVE BEST ARCHAEOLOGICAL SITES

Among the myriad prehistoric stone monuments and villages scattered across Minorca, **Trepucó** boasts the tallest *taula,* just south of Mahón. West of the capital, **Talatí de Dalt** is perhaps the prettiest of the sites. **Torre d'en Gaumés**, south of Alaior, is the largest settlement in the islands. Majorca has fewer ancient sites, but the most noteworthy is **Ses Païsses**, a collection of prehistoric dwellings and *talaiots* on the southern outskirts of Artà. See also the Roman theatre at **Alcúdia**.

tasteful examples of Mahón's characteristic English architecture. Straightforward Georgian-style houses with sash windows, elegantly simple doors—often the only concession to local traditions is the addition of shutters to keep out the blinding Mediterranean sun. At the end of the street, the Church of Sant Francesc has been renovated to house a museum displaying notably some interesting archaeological finds.

The Southeast

These excursions around the southeast corner of the island, visiting caves in the cliffs, prehistoric sites and country villages, are within easy reach of Mahón or the holiday resorts along the coast.

Es Castell (Villacarlos)

At the eastern end of the harbour, 3 km (less than 2 miles) from Mahón, the neatly planned little village has changed its name from Georgetown (after King George III), but the town hall has retained an undeniably English air.

Originally built for families of the 18th-century garrison at Fort Marlborough, the castle (also renamed, Sant Felipe) has been reduced to a ruin. On the waterfront, caves once used by fishermen have been transformed into restaurants and bars.

Trepucó

South of Mahón, this prehistoric settlement claims the biggest *taula* on the island. A massive granite slab stands 4 m (13 ft) high, with another slab 3.75 m (12 ft 4 in) long and 1.84 m (6 ft) wide placed on top like a table for the gods. Among the many interpretations of its original purpose, scholars suggest that the monument erected in the middle of a circular wall of stones served as a funeral platform exposing the deceased for cremation or some other sacrificial ritual. It stands in a village of *talaiot* mounds and dwellings that perhaps date to 1200 BC.

Sant Lluís

Down the road from Trepucó, this town was founded by the French, from the time of their occupation of the island during the Seven Years War (1756–63). The layout of small houses clustered around the parish church with an attractive baroque façade is classically French. But the immaculate whitewash of the houses and windmills roundabout are unmistakably Minorcan.

Holiday Villages

Dazzling white, self-contained holiday villages—Punta Prima, Binibeca Vell, Cala'n Porter—have sprung up along the southeast coast, complete with shops, bars, restaurants, launderettes and sports facilities. Some of the developments have made an honourable effort to reproduce traditional fishermen's houses—Binibeca Vell, in particular. Most of the beaches are accessible by stairways; wide and gently shelving, they are ideal for families with children.

Caves

The prehistoric users of the caves just east of Cala'n Porter would be justifiably amazed at what has happened to them today. Named, says the legend, after a North African pirate who made it his hideout, Cova d'en Xoroi has been transformed into a bar by day and disco by night. The view is terrific.

More than 100 man-made grottoes make up Cales Coves. They served as burial chambers around 800 BC but are now very much the preserve of the living, housing holidaymakers from latterday hippies to local Minorcan picnickers.

The North

More rugged than the south and west, the north offers windswept landscapes as you head from Mahón to the coast. A pair of binoculars will be useful to spot the birdlife on the way.

THE NORTH

S'Albufera
On the marshy shores of a charming little lake due north of Mahón, this nature reserve was saved from the clutches of an over-eager resort-developer by a nationwide ecological campaign. Flocks of osprey, heron, cormorant and spoonbill gather in a friendly wilderness of dwarf pine and juniper. Bordering a lagoon among narrow channels of reedy waterways, the nearby resort of Es Grau has a sandy beach and a couple of good harbourfront restaurants.

Fornells
Drop the l's and pronounce it *Fornez*. It is the best known of the northern resorts, indeed the only real sheltered sea-port along the mostly inaccessible coast. The local fishing industry slumbers, but tourism thrives, with well-run resort developments in the vicinity. Water sports enthusiasts say the area offers the island's best conditions for windsurfing.

For a good view, climb up to the 18th-century watchtower on Cape Fornells. The harbour itself is particularly appreciated

The dazzling holiday village of Binibeca Vell.

for its seafood restaurants serving the local delicacy, *caldereta*. King Juan Carlos sails into port to taste the lobster version of this garlicky stew, but lesser Minorcan mortals favour a variation with mixed shellfish and white fish, just as good and much cheaper.

Cap de Cavalleria

Northernmost point of the island, the barren promontory buffeted by the winds plunges 90 m (300 ft) down to the sea. The view along the coast is invigorating. From the road to the cliff-edge, you walk among the sparse ruins of what was once the Carthaginian and Roman port city of Sanisera, now known as Sa Nitja.

The Centre

The east-west road across the island was one of the major gifts of 18th-century British colonization. The modern highway from Mahón runs parallel to the more picturesque *Camí d'en Kane* named after its much admired builder, Governor Richard Kane. To take the governor's old country road, follow the signposts to Fornells and take the left turn onto Camí d'en Kane. It joins up with the modern highway just past Alaior.

The drive takes you close to several prehistoric monuments and the island's only mountain, and in general gives you a comfortable view of the countryside bathed in that unique Minorcan light.

Talatí de Dalt

Signposted just off the highway west of Mahón, this group of *taulas* and *talaiots* amidst the meadows is one of the most at-

---

THE SIX BEST BEACHES On Majorca, if you don't mind the crowds but do like a pretty setting of pine trees, **Illetes** is a popular choice among the Bay of Palma's sandy beaches. Most spectacular of Majorca's coves is **Sa Calobra** with beaches of smooth white pebbles. Over on the northeast peninsula, try the pine-shaded **Platja de Formentor**. On the south coast, nudists head for **Es Trenc**. Among Minorca's sandy beaches, the seemingly endless expanse of **Son Bou** is a family favourite. **Algaiarens**, near Cala Morell, is the best bathing beach on the northwest coast.

tractive prehistoric sites on the island. Try to visit it early in the morning or at sunset when the stone takes on a pink or golden hue.

At the centre of a horseshoe-shaped sanctuary, the main T-shaped *taula* has a second one leaning against it as a massive prop. There are also several hypostyle (columned) halls, and burial chambers hewn from caves in a nearby hill.

Torralba d'en Salort

The prehistoric stonemason's art is beautifully demonstrated in this well-preserved ancient settlement, just off the Alaior–Cala en Porter road south of the main highway. Giant slabs have been hewn and meticulously shaped both as *taulas* and as the walls of *talaiot* shrines set in natural caves. Scholars date the monuments around 900 BC.

Alaior

The town is known for its dairy products, a respectable ice cream and excellent *coinga* cheeses. Taste both while you are here, ideally at the Thursday market. With its gleaming white houses strategically located on a low hill in the middle of the plain, the town (pronounced locally *Aló*) was built in the 14th century to guard the route between Mahón and Ciutadella.

The two main churches, Sant Diego and Santa Eulària, both 17th-century, stand at the top of the town and provide excellent viewpoints down to the south coast.

Torre d'en Gaumés

This is the largest of the prehistoric settlements in the Balearic Islands, and one of the most impressive. South of the cross-island highway, it lies at the end of a beautiful country lane off the Alaior–Son Bou road. The complex of columned halls, houses, sanctuary walls and burial chambers has been dated back to 1500 BC. With their unimpeded view down to the sea, the imposing *talaiots* were almost certainly watchtowers. Among the megaliths, notice some that have been hollowed out as water troughs or ritual fonts, or perhaps for settling sediment in water before running it off into cisterns.

Platja de Son Bou

The long stretch of white sandy beach, both dunes and flats, makes this a favourite for families. Away from the big resort, the quieter salt marshes attract migratory birds. Close to the sea at the east end of the beach, an early Christian basilica has recently been excavated to reveal the remains of a narthex (entrance hall) that had three portals leading to the three-aisle church with a semi-circular apse. Notice, too, the imposing baptismal font.

Monte Toro

As mountains go, it's not much, 357 m (1,170 ft), but it's all they've got, so at least there is nothing around to block the view from the top. From Mercadal— where the only reason to stop is to sample the town's justly famous macaroons, *macarrons dulces*—a winding road takes you up to the Franciscan church and monastery. The panorama covers the whole island and gives you a wonderful sense of a neat English patchwork of country meadows, walled off by Minorcan stone in an unmistakably Mediterranean light. In the church courtyard, refresh yourself with the ice-cold water from the well. At the summit, a huge modern statue of Jesus erected to commemorate the victims of the Spanish Civil War has to contend with a barrage of antennae and satellite dishes.

Ciutadella

When the British moved the island's administration from Ciutadella to Mahón in the 18th century, the aristocrats and the princes of the church stayed behind. The British are long gone (except for the holidaymakers), but the town has retained its stately, conservative cachet. The cathedral, bishop's palace and the nobles' mansions are still there, most affirmatively Spanish, with none of the English architectural trimmings you see on the other side of the island.

Plaça Alfons III

The cross-island highway enters town at the lively square from which broad avenues branch out along the path of the ancient Roman and Moorish city ram-

---

SAUCY MINORCA

The British may dollop more of it on their salads than the French, but mayonnaise, believed to have started here as *mahonesa,* was most likely to have been a contribution of the French during their occupation of Minorca from 1756 to 1763. Duke Louis François Armand de Richelieu, the cardinal's grand-nephew, brutal soldier and lusty libertine, claims to have created the sauce in an idle moment between battlefield and boudoir. Certainly, the necessary ingredients were all available on the island—high-quality olive oil, egg yolks and mustard-seed. And the brisk whipping essential for its ideal concoction was indeed a favourite pastime of the duke.

CIUTADELLA

Castell de Sant Nicolau is all that remains of Ciutadella's fortifications.

parts, *Sa Contramurada,* removed at the end of the 19th century. At its north end, Bastió de Sa Font houses the municipal museum.

Ses Voltes
The main street leading through the old town from Plaça Alfons III begins as Carrer Maó and takes, after Plaça Nova, the official name of local historian, Josep M. Quadrado. But it is known to everyone simply as *Ses Voltes* (The Arches) for the Moorish-style arcades providing welcome shade as you stroll past the boutiques, jewellery shops, bakeries and cafés.

The terraces of Plaça Nova are a good spot to investigate the local ice cream or deliciously sweet *ensaimada* pastries.

Cathedral
From the opposite shore of the narrow harbour you can consider the sturdy fortress-like silhouette of the cathedral. Founded in the 13th century, after conquest of the island by King Alfonso III, it was built and rebuilt with much of the masonry of the mosque it replaced. The burnt-out shell left by the Turks in 1558 was restored to its present Gothic form over the next 300 years. Beautifully lit by narrow win-

dows set high in the walls, the choir displays the most elaborate ornamentation in an otherwise sober interior.

The two huge bells in the tower are rung with great gusto on the town's Feast of St John in June.

Old Town Houses

Some handsome examples of aristocratic mansions can be seen along Carrer Sant Sebastià immediately east of the cathedral, notably the 18th-century Italian-style Palau de Can Squella. South of the cathedral, on Carrer del Santissim, is the balconied façade of the 17th-century Palau de Martorell.

Leading from the southern corner of Plaça de la Catedral, the more modest houses of the old Jewish Quarter *(Es Call)* are to be found around Sant Jeroni, Sant Frances and Palau streets.

Plaça d'Es Born

It is easy to imagine the broad open square serving originally as the parade ground for the island's Moorish rulers—Ciutadella's talented black horses perform here during the June festivities for St John's Day. The square is surrounded today by the majestic town palaces of the aristocracy, built mostly in the 19th century and partaking even here of that pompous but nonetheless impressive atmosphere known elsewhere as Victorian. The platoons of puffed up pigeons seem to understand.

On the west side of the square, a peep inside the Ajuntament (town hall), with the lofty coffered ceilings of its ceremonial chambers, will give you some idea of Ciutadella's self-image. The other houses on the square are not open to the public, but for a fuller sense of the grandeur, if not folly, of the old aristocracy, you can take a tour of Palau Salort, just off the square on Carrer Major del Born.

The obelisk in the centre of the square was erected in 1857 to commemorate the disaster of the Turkish conquest.

Plaça de S'Esplanada

This even larger rectangular square is more popular with the townsfolk of Ciutadella. Lined with pine trees, it is the setting for concerts, election meetings, second-hand book fairs and that ubiquitous Mediterranean sport of *petanca,* the Spanish version of French *boules* or Italian *boccie.*

Connoisseurs note that Minorcans bring an almost mystic concentration to the game, muttering dark, not necessarily religious imprecations as they bomb their opponent's ball—triumphing without the slightest hint of a smile.

CIUTADELLA • WESTERN BEACHES

The Port
Ciutadella's narrow inlet proved an attractive sheltered harbour for shipping throughout the Middle Ages, until the bigger vessels of the 18th century required more space and turned to Mahon's deeper anchorage. But the port remained an attractive haven for fishing vessels. The caves that the fishermen carved out of the cliffs below the old fortifications have today been transformed into restaurants, bars and night clubs. The Ciutadella Yacht Club stages regattas here throughout the year. The long Pla de Sant Joan that comes down to the water's edge at the mouth of the inlet is the scene of games, races and the grand *corregudes* horse parades during the St John festivities in June. For the regattas and other harbour spectacles, the terraced gardens overlooking the port become privileged loggias for viewing the events.

A dramatic summer phenomenon is the unpredictable *rissague* tide, short and sharp, which rises a full two metres higher than usual, flooding the harbour-front—or dropping by the same amount to expose the rocks of the inlet's seabed.

Castell de Sant Nicolau
At the southern end of the port, a 17th-century octagonal tower is the last substantial vestige of the town's fortifications. Its moat has been converted into public gardens. On the square opposite is a statue of American Civil War hero, Admiral David Farragut, scion of a Minorcan family which emigrated to Tennessee in the 18th century.

Western Beaches
Most of the beaches around Ciutadella at the western end of the island occupy appealing pine-shaded coves, sheltered from the winds of the open sea. They are not all easily accessible by road, so the best way to get there is by excursion boats from the resort hotels and Ciutadella itself. The overland route southeast from Ciutadella passes by the picturesque 14th-century church of Sant Joan de Missa.

Points to explore from the various beaches: at Cap d'Artrutx, see the lighthouse on the southwest tip of the island; from the long beach of Son Saura, you can visit the prehistoric village of Son Catlar; at Cala Turqueta, cool off with a walk in the pine forest; the cliffs of Cala Macarella have caves that were once Stone Age dwellings.

On the northwest coast, popular resorts take advantage of superb beaches at Cala Morell, with its prehistoric cave dwellings in the cliffs, and Algaiarens framed by dense pine woods.

Balearics from A to Z

Arabs
The name is erroneously applied to the islands' Islamic invaders, more commonly known as Moors—a mixture of North African Berbers with their Semitic Arab conquerors.

Balearic Islands
Majorca and Minorca plus the smaller islands of Ibiza and Formentera, comprising an autonomous region of Spain with its capital at Palma.

Barbarossa
Nickname of the red-bearded pirate Khair ed-Din, 16th-century scourge of the Mediterranean, including Mahón; he was made an admiral of the Turkish navy.

Carthaginians
Dynamic traders from colonies in North Africa, but originally from Lebanon, they were among early invaders of the Balearics.

Catalan
Language and culture of Catalonia, embracing the Balearic Islands. The language, descended from Latin, is the mother tongue of millions of people as far afield as parts of France and Sardinia.

Dragons
Popular monsters in Majorca, notably in the caves of Drac, but the "dragon" in Palma's Diocesan Museum is a moth-eaten alligator.

Falange
Spanish fascist party of the 1930s invoking imperial and traditional Christian values, strong in Majorca, resisted in Minorca.

Fiestas
Biggest and best: Palma's *Sant Pere* in June and Valldemossa's *Santa Catalina* in July; Ciutadella's *Sant Joan* (John) in June and Mahón's *Festa del Carme* in July.

Graves, Robert (1895–1985)
English writer and poet, author of *I, Claudius,* long exiled and buried in Deià (Majorca).

Knights of St John
Descendants of the Crusaders established a garrison in Pollença in the 18th century.

Llull, Ramón
Palma's eclectic 13th-century church scholar, Majorca's greatest intellectual figure, who dabbled in philosophy, mysticism, alchemy and poetry.

Miró, Joan (1893–1983)
The Paris-trained abstract surrealist painter spent the last half of his life in Palma, home of his mother's family.

Moors
Islamic people of Arab and North African Berber stock. They occupied much of Spain for more than seven centuries.

Moriscos
Muslims converted to Christianity after the *Reconquista* but many of them remained secretly faithful to Islam.

Navetas
Prehistoric stone burial halls shaped like upturned ship's hull.

Paseo
Daily social event, the evening promenade along the sea front or through a town square.

Pirates
From Islamic Barbary states, Morocco, Algeria, Tunisia and Libya, but not infrequently from Christian Spain, too.

Reconquista
The crusade to reconquer Spain from the Moors became a campaign of ethnic purification in 1492 with the expulsion or conversion of Muslims and Jews.

Talaiot
Prehistoric stone mound of undetermined purpose—perhaps they were erected for funeral rites or simply to serve as watch-towers.

Taula
Prehistoric T-shaped megalith found mainly in Minorca, perhaps for ritual sacrifice or burial platform.

Vandals
Ancient invaders of Germanic origin. Their name is synonymous with destruction, but they probably built the "Roman" bridge at Pollença.

Windmills
They irrigate the Majorca plain by pumping the underground springs that are believed to flow all the way beneath the Mediterranean from the Pyrenees.

Ximbombas
Bawdy folk songs in local dialect.

Xuetos (or Chuetos)
The Jewish equivalent of *Moriscos*, converts to Christianity continuing clandestine fidelity to Judaism.

Zarzuela
Spanish light opera performed at Palma's Teatre Principal—and also the name of a tasty seafood casserole.

Shopping

Traditional crafts and skills are fighting a valiant back-to-the-wall battle of survival, but they haven't lost yet. Next to the time-honoured arts of basket-weaving and work in leather, jewellery, ceramics, brass and copper, the manufacture of top-quality artificial pearls is a relative newcomer. Add to that the smart silks and satins in the boutiques of downtown Palma and delicacies from the islands' gourmet shops and wine-cellars, and you'll find plenty of gifts for family, friends and yourself.

Where?
In the realm of shopping, Palma's big-city status really makes itself felt. The boutiques for high fashion on Avinguda del Rei Jaume III and Carrer Jaume II stand comparison with any in Spain. The pedestrian shopping zone between Plaça Major and Plaça Cort is especially good for jewellery and table linen. You might find a wider range of leather or other crafted goods in the factory showrooms or workshops, but the prices will not necessarily be better. Plaça Major holds a craft market on Friday and Saturday. Other markets: Sunday at Alcúdia, Wednesday at Andratx and Port de Pollença. The model farm and open-air craft museum at La Granja offers a wide range of folk art and nicely packaged country cookery.

On Minorca, Mahón is best for silverware, Alaior for copper and brassware. Ciutadella, holding its market on Saturday, is good for ceramics.

What?
Whatever it is you decide to buy, make sure you can *carry* it home. Avoid fragile glass and ceramics—luckily most of the local craftware is quite sturdy. In any case, it is best not to rely on the islands' package and postal system. Shop around before buying. And you're on your own when it comes to distinguishing the genuine product from the fake.

Craftware
The local embroidered table and bed linen is attractive. The simplest designs in hand-woven basketware are the best; consider

a straw hat to set you apart from the mob of baseball caps. The quaint ceramic figurines known as *siurells,* with a whistle in the top, are among the oldest artefacts in the islands, their design dating back to the ancient Phoenicians. Yes, they are phallic, they always were. They are put on the bedside table of newly-weds as a talisman.

For more traditional pottery, especially for the kitchen, try the Felanitx workshops in southern Majorca or the dark glazed ceramics of Inca.

Besides its pearls, Manacor is reviving the craft of olive wood carving for utensils and ornaments.

Jewellery

The silver- and goldsmiths of Palma and Mahón continue a centuries-old tradition. Their work, particularly in the mounting of precious stones, is of the highest quality. And in this age of quartz crystals and plastic throwaways, Palma's jewellers still repair handmade watches—and occasionally have an interesting antique model for sale. Less élitist is the thriving trade in artificial pearls manufactured at Manacor in Majorca's heartland. The now famous pearls are created from tiny glass beads covered with a paste of fish scales and resin, but only those Palma jewellers could tell the difference from the real thing.

Leatherware

Only the heaviest luggage is made from last year's bullfights. Most of the goods, whether handbags, jackets or other leather and suede clothing, are made from the finest, soft and supple hides. For shoes, you will get better bargains at the top of the range. Children's shoes are particularly good. For your excursions, try a pair of *avarques*—lightweight summer shoes. On Majorca, you can visit the factories in Inca, buy from their showrooms or wait till you get back to Palma to compare prices. On Minorca, the best selections of shoes are in Alaior and Ciutadella.

Gourmet Gifts

You might like to take home some Majorca sausage *(sobrasada)*, Minorca cheeses or a box of sweetmeats—marzipan, *amargos* bitter almond, or little *besitos* "kisses". And besides the lusty Spanish brandy, surprise your friends with Majorca's almond-flavoured liqueur.

Musical Instruments

If you develop a taste for *flamenco* and Spanish music in general, Ciutadella is the place to buy a well-crafted guitar or other traditional instrument. *Olé!*

Sports

For some people, sports are the only reason for coming to the islands in the first place. Most of them will be so absorbed by the profusion of facilities for sports in and out of the water that they will find little time to read these few lines. For the rest, here are a few pointers as to what is available.

Water Sports

For swimming, the beaches range from long stretches of white sands gently sloping down to the sea around Majorca's bays of Palma and Pollença or Minorca's Son Bou, to little rocky coves and creeks, both sandy and smooth pebble, providing shelter from the wind and rough seas. Windsurfers don't worry about such things and go for the gusty open sea off Fornells on Minorca or the north coast resorts of Majorca—rentals are available at every resort. Water-skiing and paragliding are big on the Bay of Palma.

Sailing enthusiasts are spoiled, at last count, by no less than 23 marinas or yachting harbours on the big island. Boats also ferry holidaymakers around the coasts as the easiest way of visiting secluded beaches.

Snorkelling and scuba-diving are superlative at Ratjada and Sa Calobra. Major hotels in these resorts also provide professional training and equipment for deep-sea diving.

Fishing

If dawn is too early for your holiday fishing, you can always angle off the jetty while watching the sun set, another good meal time for the fish. Licences are issued at the Commandancia de Marina in Palma harbour. Or hire a boat for night-time fishing with a good chance of catching tuna. Freshwater fishing at the Gorg Blau reservoir between Sóller and Sa Calobra offers trout and carp.

Golf and Tennis

Your travel agency or hotel can advise about temporary membership at Majorca's golf clubs—18-hole courses in beautiful coastal settings at Son Vida, Magalluf and Santa Ponça. Minorca has a 13-hole course at Son Parc on the north coast. Many of the hotels have their own tennis courts, but

After your hike, you'll soon find a beach to cool off.

you will find better surfaces at club courts in Palma, Mahón and Ciutadella.

Hiking

The walking is easier—flatter—on Minorca and an excellent way to visit the prehistoric settlements of *taulas* and *talaiots* and at the same time discover the countryside. People who like the tougher terrain of Majorca's Tramuntana mountains can get trail maps and guidance from the tourist office in Sóller.

Spectator Sports

Even if you like bullfights, you should know that Spanish *aficionados* do not rate highly the summer Sunday-afternoon spectacle at Palma's Plaça de Toros. The arena is divided into three areas: *sol,* the almost unbearable sunny side, *sombra,* the more comfortable and understandably more expensive shady side, and the *sol y sombra,* combining the two without having the sun directly in your eyes.

There is less blood but equally fierce excitement for the summer weekend harness racing at horse tracks, most colourfully on Minorca in Ciutadella and Mahón, but also staged on Majorca at Son Pardo (north of Palma) and Manacor.

Dining Out

Although most resort hotels are content to serve "international" fare, sooner or later even the most hardened home-style-meat-and-potatoes people may like to venture out and try the local cuisine. Follow the islanders away from the resorts to the towns of the interior—Inca, Calvià, Binissalem and Bunyola in Majorca or Mercadal and Alaior in Minorca.

To Start With...

You can try out a lot of the appetizers as lunchtime *tapas* in bars and cafés. These snacks may be hot or cold: shrimps, meatballs, potato salad, marinated squid or fresh anchovy, olives, grilled red peppers, or a slice of omelette (*tortilla*) made with onions and potatoes.

One of the most simple starters is *pa amb oli*, bread with olive oil, crushed tomato, garlic and capers. *Sopes mallorquines* (Majorcan soup) is a great filler, closer to a stew than soup, adding pieces of pork to aubergine (eggplant), cauliflower and other vegetables and flavoured with olive oil and garlic. You get a thick chunk of country bread for soaking up the soup.

Main Course: Fish or Meat?

The demand for fish is so heavy that much of it has to be brought in from ports as distant as Spain's Atlantic coast, and thus it often arrives frozen rather than fresh. *Lampuga* is a strictly local fish. Other options: grouper served with bacon (*anfós amb xulla*), red mullet (*salmonete*), eel (*anguila*), tuna (*bonito*), and red spiny lobster (*langosta*) starring in the Minorcan *caldereta* fish-stew cooked up in Fornells. Trout (*trucha*) is a rare delicacy from Majorca's reservoirs. A Majorcan fish-stew (*zarzuela de mariscos*) is clearly Moorish in inspiration with its sweet and sour sauce mixing tomatoes, onions, raisins and almonds. On Minorca, British visitors will find something familiar about the local name for the fish-sauce—*grevi*.

A favourite among the islands' meat dishes is the roast suckling pig (*porcela rostida*) brought in

There's plenty to choose from if you opt for a picnic.

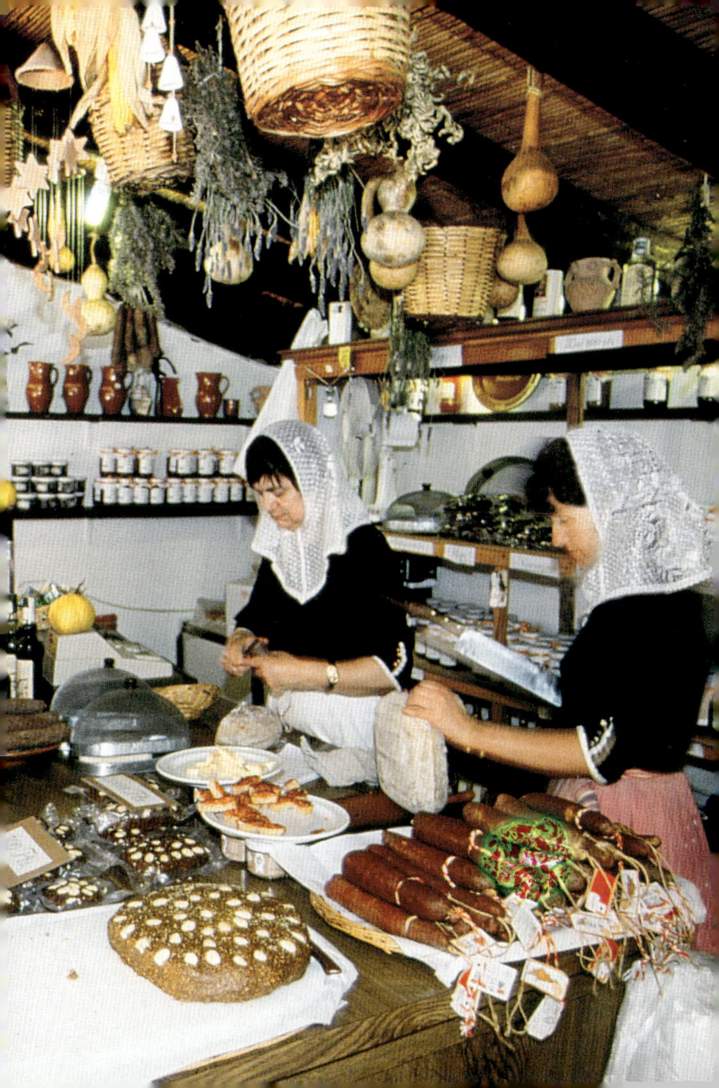

with the Reconquista by the kings of Aragon and served tender as butter. The pig is a staple of the dinner table in pork stews and casseroles, ham, sausage served with honey *(sobrasada)* or the more spicy blood sausage *(botifarró)*.

Lamb *(cordero)* may come stewed with pomegranates, or partridge *(perdriz)* with cabbage. At Easter, you may find *empanada pascual,* a lamb pie baked with a pastry of unleavened flour, an old Jewish Passover dish.

Cheese
Minorca's cheeses, from Mahón and Alaior, are highly prized, coming in two qualities—*tierno* from cow's milk, soft and creamy, or the firmer, stronger *curado,* with ewe's milk added. Great with country bread.

Desserts
The islands' favourite pastry is the airy, light *ensaimada,* a spongy spiral delight powdered with sugar and sometimes filled with cream. The more solid pies, *cocas,* have a filling of fruit or marzipan (they also exist in a savoury version with spinach, cheese or tomato and onions).

Minorca's dairy farms produce excellent ice cream with exotic flavours like prickly pear, orange-blossom, toasted almond and fig.

Drinks
The best of the islands' own wines come from Binissalem and Felanitx, the reds *(tinto)* being easier on the palate than the rather harsh whites *(blanco)*. There are few notable rosés *(rosado)*.

From mainland Spain, try the Rioja reds or Catalan *Sangre de Toro.* Bubbly *cava* is a reasonably acceptable substitute for champagne.

Jugfuls of *sangría,* that refreshing summer wine punch flavoured with cinnamon and bits of fruit, may seem as easy to drink as lemonade, but beware of the after-effects. For something more innocuous, try one of the deliciously fresh fruit juices, which you can order in any combination you fancy.

Minorca gin is remarkably good, but you may be surprised to see it bottled as a liqueur with honey *(gin-i-miel)* or with lemonade *(pomada)*. Other island liqueurs are made with various local fruit *(resolis),* carob seeds *(palo)* or aromatic herbs *(hierbas seca)*. Spanish brandy is a strong mainland concoction.

Beer drinkers need no guidance. Their own favourite home brews are available in abundance, bottled or draught, but German, British and Dutch brands are double the price of the perfectly respectable local beers, served refreshingly cold.

The Hard Facts

To plan your trip, here are some of the practical details you should know about Majorca and Minorca.

Airports
International flights come into Palma, with local connections to Mahón. Both Palma and Mahón terminals provide car-hire and tourist information office services, in addition to duty-free shop, restaurant and snack bar facilities. Palma also has banking facilities; there is a cash machine at Mahón. If you do not have special bus arrangements as part of your tour package, there are plenty of taxis, airport buses (Palma only) and public transport to take you to most of the major resort towns.

Climate
Since people discovered the delight of its mild winters, Majorca has become a year-round destination. July and August are scorchers with temperatures rising to 30°C (86°F), June and September scarcely cooler with highs only a couple of degrees less. Mellowest months are April, May and October, the time for comfortable rambles.

In the winter months, the mountains shield the south coast from the *tramuntana* winds. It does rain, but not what the British call *rain*.

Minorca does not have a mountain barrier to keep out the north winds, so its busy seasons last only from early May to the end of October.

Communications
Spain has installed a highly modern telecommunication system for fax and phone. Call worldwide with telecards from streetphones, much cheaper than the hotel's surcharge service.

Crime
Pickpockets are on the increase at the beach and in crowded places in town—very often they may be fellow tourists. Without undue paranoia, don't tempt them with an open handbag or a wallet in the hip pocket. Leave your valuables in the hotel safe. Lock your luggage before leaving it with porters at the airport.

Driving
If you are renting a car, be sure to have a valid national licence or

THE HARD FACTS

International Driving Permit. If you have not booked a car back home, you will find local rental firms very competitive in price with the major international companies. Rental age limit is usually over 21, sometimes over 25.

Speed limits are 50 kph in town and 90 kph on the highway, 120 kph on the motorways. Drive on the right, overtake on the left.

Except for a few bumpy mountain roads, Majorca's highways are in excellent condition. Minorca's Mahón-Ciutadella road is first class. Country roads may be badly paved and above all very narrow between high stone walls, but well worth the adventure.

Electric Current
Almost universally 220 volts AC, 50 Hz, with just a few older installations still using 125 volts.

Emergencies
Most problems can be handled at your hotel desk. Telephone number for police (*Guardia Civil*): **091**. Consular help is there (in Palma) only for critical situations—lost passports or worse, *not* for lost cash or plane tickets.

Essentials
Pack a sunhat and add a sweater for cool evenings. Good walking shoes are vital, especially for the mountains. Include insect repellent to deal with the occasional mosquitoes, and a torch (flashlight), and plenty of high-factor sunblock.

Formalities
A valid passport is all that most visitors need—or an identity card for members of EC countries.

Customs controls are minimal at point of entry, with an official import allowance for visitors from countries outside the EU of the following quantities, duty-free: 200 cigarettes or 50 cigars or 250 g tobacco, 1 litre spirits over 22°, 2 litres up to 22° and 2 litres other wines.

There is no limit on the quantity of goods purchased *duty-paid* in another EU country, provided they are for personal use only. There are no restrictions on the amount of local or foreign currencies imported or exported if you are coming from another EU country; otherwise amounts exceeding 10,000 Euro or equivalent must be declared.

Certain prescription medications may require an official medical certificate.

Health
There are no special health problems you can blame on the islands. Most casualties are from too much sun or *sangría*. As everywhere these days, avoid excessive direct exposure to that Mediterranean heat. In case of

accident or illness, holiday health insurance is strongly recommended. Doctors, dentists and hospital staff are of generally good standard, many speaking some English. If you take prescription medicines, pack enough of your own, as you may not find the exact equivalent on the spot.

Holidays and festivals
Public holidays in Majorca and Minorca are of both historical and religious significance:

January 1	New Year
January 6	Epiphany
March 1	Balearic Islands Day
May 1	Labour Day
July 25	St James
August 15	Assumption
October 12	National holiday
November 1	All Saints' Day
December 6	Constitution Day
December 8	Immaculate Conception
December 25	Christmas
December 26	Boxing Day

Movable: Maundy Thursday, Good Friday, Easter Monday.

Languages
Majorcans and Minorcans speak the *Mallorquín* or *Menorquín* version of Catalan, as well as Castilian Spanish. Many if not most Majorcans speak either English or German and sometimes French, too. On Minorca, the dominant second language is English.

Media
British and other European newspapers and the *International Herald Tribune* and *Wall Street Journal* come into Palma on the date of publication. Majorca publishes a local English-language daily. Many hotels have satellite-dish reception for BBC, CNN and other non-Spanish TV.

Money
The euro. Shops and restaurants accept credit cards and travellers cheques, but smaller establishments prefer cash. Cash-distributors are available in Palma and other sizeable towns.

Opening Hours
In general, **shops** and **offices** open 9 a.m.–1 p.m., latest 2 p.m., before the siesta begins. Depending on the season, the heat or other imponderable, they re-open at 4 or 5 p.m. and close around 8 p.m. **Big supermarkets** stay open at lunchtime.

Banks open in Majorca Monday to Friday 8.30 a.m.– 1.30 p.m. (2.30 p.m. in winter), Saturday 9 a.m.–1 p.m. (may vary in smaller towns); Minorca Monday to Friday 8.30 a.m.–2 p.m.

Restaurants serve lunch from 1 p.m. to about 3.30 p.m. and dinner from as early as 7 p.m. for tourist restaurants, but not until 8.30 p.m. in places for the Spanish population.

▶ THE HARD FACTS

Photography
Choose speeds for the brilliant Mediterranean light. Photography may be forbidden around parts of Palma airport or military installations on Puig Major and at Port de Sóller.

Public Transport
Majorca has a good daily bus service, with special shuttle services in summer from Palma to and from the major beaches. Main starting points are Plaça de la Reina and Plaça Espanya. Sóller serves its port with a grand old tramway. Minorca's buses run less frequently but do link the main towns. The Mahón bus station is at Plaça Esplanada.

The narrow-gauge train crossing the mountains from Palma to Sóller is an experience in itself. Take the 10.40 a.m. for its midday stop up in the mountains. Another train runs to Inca.

Social Graces
The islanders are friendly enough, but tend to be much more reserved than you might have imagined. The year-round presence of tourists has accustomed them to boisterous behaviour. They shake hands but don't hug half as much as other Latins might. They may be pleasantly surprised to hear you greet them with a *bon dia* or *bona tarda*. And however casually dressed or underdressed you might be for the beach or the café, remember to cover yourself decently when entering a church.

Time
The Balearics are switched to the same time as mainland Spain: GMT + 1 in winter, GMT + 2 in summer.

Tipping
Service is included in restaurant and hotel bills, shared among the whole staff, but an extra 5 or 10 per cent is customary.

Toilets
When a little male or female figure does not indicate which is which, you should know that the women's room is usually marked by an "S" *(Señoras)* and the men's by a "C" *(Caballeros)*. Public toilets are a rarity, but if you use the facilities in a bar or restaurant, it is customary to order at least a drink there. Ask for the *servicios* or *aseos*.

Tourist Information Offices
There are tourist information centres on Majorca in Palma, Pollença, Sóller and major beach resorts, and in Mahón. They provide maps and brochures in English, French and German, particularly useful for ramblers' nature trails and tracking down elusive prehistoric sites.

Mahón (Maó)

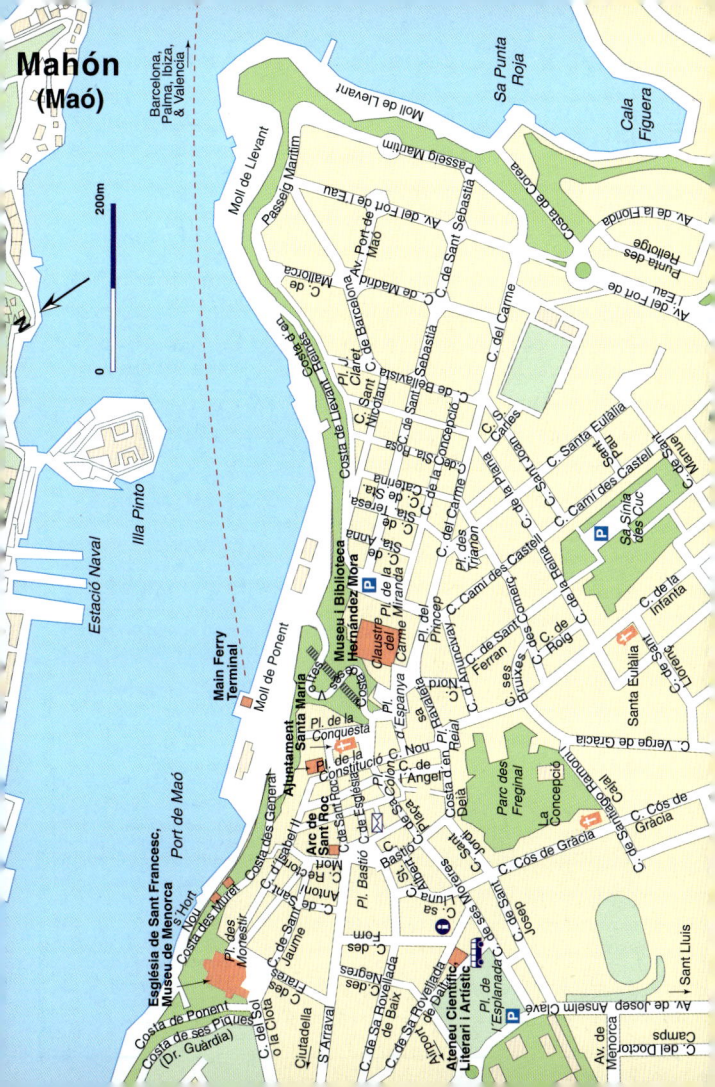

INDEX

Majorca
Alaró Castle 30
Alcúdia 32
Alfàbia Mansion 30
Andratx, Port d' 23
Artà 34–35
Artà, Coves de 35
Banyalbufar 24
Bellver Castle 19–20
Biniraix 28
Binissalem 36
Ca'n Picafort 33
Cala d'Or 34
Cala Figuera 34
Cala Fornells 23
Cala Ratjada 35
Capdepera 35
Capocorp Vell 36
Deià 26–28
Drac, Coves del 33
Dragonera, Illa de 23–24
Es Trenc 36
Estallencs 24
Felanitx 36
Formentor 31–32
Fornalutx 28
Hams, Coves dels 33
Illetes 21
Inca 36
La Granja 24–25
Les Meravelles 21
Lluc Monastery 29–30
Magaluf 22
Palma 15–21
Peguera 23
Pollença 30–31
Pollença, Port de 31
Portals Nous 21–22
Porto Colom 33–34
Porto Cristo 33
S'Albufera 32
S'Arenal 21
Sa Calobra 28
Sa Cartuja 25–26
Sant Telm 23
Santa Ponça 23
Ses Païsses 34
Sóller 28
Sóller, Port de 28
Son Marroig 26
Valldemossa 25

Minorca
Alaior 45
Algaiarens 44
Artrutx, Cap d' 49
Binibeca Vell 41–42
Cala'n Porter 41
Cales Coves 42
Cavalleria, Cap de 44
Ciutadella 46–49
Es Castell 41
Fornells 43–44
Mahón (Maó) 39–41
Monte Toro 17, 46
Punta Prima 41
S'Albufera 43
Sant Lluís 43
Son Bou, Platja de 45–46
Talatí de Dalt 44–45
Torralba d'en Salort 45
Torre d'en Gaumés 45
Trepucó 41
Villacarlos 41
Xoroi, Cova d'en 42

GENERAL EDITOR
Barbara Ender-Jones
LAYOUT
Luc Malherbe
PHOTO CREDITS
Huber/Schmid, except:
Corbis/Rossenbach: p. 2
istockphoto.com/Lingbeek: p. 13; /Winkler: p. 22; /Gülden pp. 34–35
hemis.fr/Wysocki: p. 27
Adverta AG Vaduz: p. 55
MAPS
Elsner & Schichor;
JPM Publications

Copyright © 2008, 1996
by JPM Publications S.A.
12, avenue William-Fraisse,
1006 Lausanne, Switzerland
information@jpmguides.com
http://www.jpmguides.com/

All rights reserved. No part of this book may be reproduced or transmitted in any form or by any means, electronic or mechanical, including photocopying, recording or by any information storage and retrieval system without permission in writing from the publisher.

Every care has been taken to verify the information in the guide, but neither the publisher nor his client can accept responsibility for any errors that may have occurred. If you spot an inaccuracy or a serious omission, please let us know.

Printed in Switzerland
Weber Benteli/Bienne
10055.00.3980
Edition 2008–2009

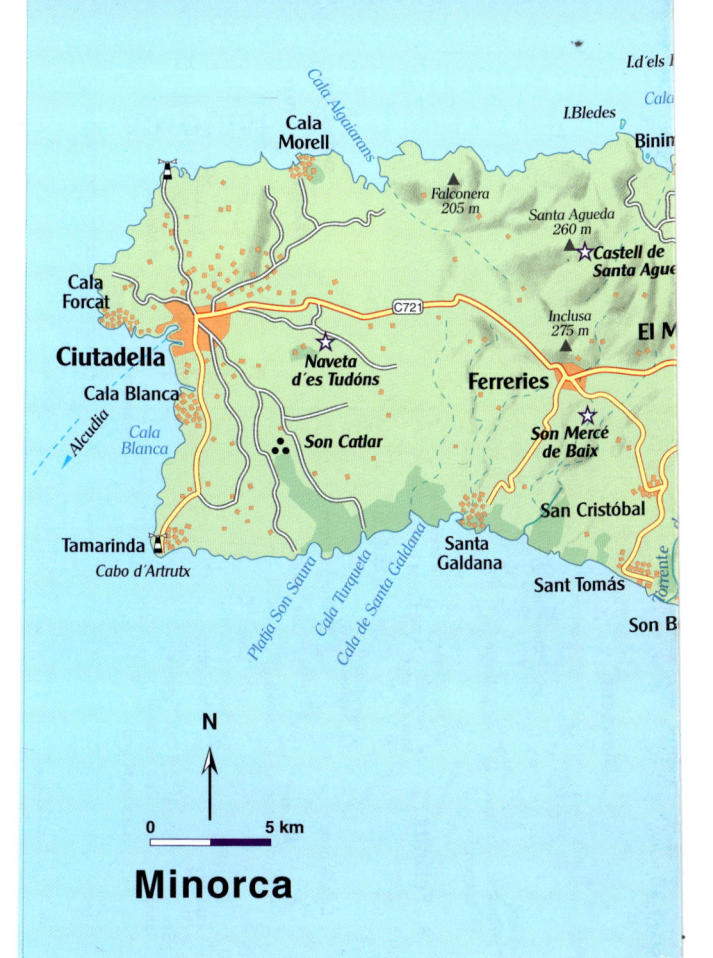

Minorca

Map labels:

- Cala Morell
- Cala Algaiarens
- I. Bledes
- Binim...
- Falconera 205 m
- Santa Agueda 260 m
- Castell de Santa Agueda
- Cala Forcat
- Ciutadella
- C721
- Inclusa 275 m
- El M...
- Cala Blanca
- Naveta d'es Tudóns
- Ferreries
- Alcudia
- Cala Blanca
- Son Catlar
- Son Mercé de Baix
- San Cristóbal
- Tamarinda
- Cabo d'Artrutx
- Platja Son Saura
- Cala Turqueta
- Cala de Santa Galdana
- Santa Galdana
- Sant Tomás
- Son B...
- Torrente...

N ↑

0 — 5 km

MAJORCA
MINORCA

More than just an island of beaches and nonstop nightlife, Majorca is rich in history and a diversity of off-beat attractions. From Palma's splendid Gothic cathedral to stunning seascapes, the sightseeing is a worthwhile break from holiday hedonism. Minorca attracts a quieter crowd, charmed by the rolling meadows, the archaeological sites and the rare convergence of civilizations.

This Way Majorca and Minorca gives you a compact introduction to the culture and beauty of this unlikely pair of Balearic islands.

- **HISTORY**
- **CULTURE**
- **MUSEUMS**
- **MONUMENTS**
- **BEACHES**
- **SHOPPING**
- **SPORTS**
- **DINING OUT**
- **PRACTICAL INFORMATION**
- **FOLD-OUT MAP**

ISBN 978-2-88452-029-4

www.JPMGuides.com